Beckett

By the same authors

MACRUNE'S GUEVARA
by John Spurling

THE NOVELS OF SAMUEL BECKETT

SAMUEL BECKETT'S ART

NEW DIRECTIONS IN LITERATURE

A CRITICAL COMMENTARY ON FLAUBERT'S
TROIS CONTES

SAMUEL BECKETT, HIS WORKS AND HIS CRITICS
(with Raymond Federman)

SAMUEL BECKETT: FIN DE PARTIE
(with Beryl S. Fletcher)

SAMUEL BECKETT: WAITING FOR GODOT
(educational edition)

FORCES IN MODERN FRENCH DRAMA
(symposium)

by John Fletcher

Beckett

A STUDY OF HIS PLAYS

by

JOHN FLETCHER
and
JOHN SPURLING

A DRAMABOOK

HILL AND WANG　NEW YORK

A division of Farrar, Straus and Giroux

Contents

Illustrations

6　HAPPY DAYS: original production by Alan Schneider at the Cherry Lane Theatre, New York, September 1961; Ruth White (*Winnie*); John C. Becher (Willie)
(*Photo: Miss Alix Jeffry*)

7　PLAY: National Theatre production by George Devine at the Old Vic Theatre, London, April 1964; Rosemary Harris, Billie Whitelaw, Robert Stephens
(*Photo: Zoe Dominic*)

8a　COME AND GO: original production by Deryk Mendel at the Schiller Theater, Berlin, September 1965; Lieselotte Rau (*Flo*); Charlotte Joeres (*Vi*); Sibylle Gilles (*Ru*)
(*Photo: Ilse Buhs*)

b　SAMUEL BECKETT with the tramps from *Waiting for Godot*
(*Photo: Roger Pic*)

The cartoon of *Endgame* by Vicky on p. 46 is reproduced from the New Statesman (31 July 1964) by permission; the cartoon by Vicky of *Waiting for Godot* is reproduced on p. 146 by arrangement with the trustees and the Evening Standard © London Express; the photomontage of *Play* reproduced on p. 113 is by courtesy of the Industrial Development Authority of Ireland.

Foreword

We have composed this essay (which stresses throughout Beckett's success as an innovator in the theatre) in close collaboration. John Fletcher wrote the Chronology, Chapters 3, 5, 7, 8 and 11, and John Spurling the rest.

Norwich and London, January 1971

J. F.
J. S.

AUTHORS' ACKNOWLEDGEMENTS

We are grateful to Samuel Beckett, Roger Blin and Alan Schneider for kindly providing us with useful information. For permission to make quotations from his published works, thanks are due to Mr Beckett, Messrs Faber and Faber Ltd and Calder and Boyars Ltd, London, and Grove Press Inc., New York. A xerox copy of *Eleuthéria* was kindly made available by the University of California (Santa Barbara) Library, and quotations (translated by John Spurling, amended by Samuel Beckett) were taken from it by courtesy of the author and Editions de Minuit, Paris. Illustrations are reproduced by permission.

Samuel Barclay Beckett

1906 Born at Foxrock near Dublin on 13 April (Good Friday), second son of William Frank Beckett, a quantity surveyor, and his wife Mary, *née* Roe. Middle-class Protestant family, comfortably off. Kindergarten: Miss Ida Elsner's Academy, Stillorgan. Prep. school: Earlsfort House School, Dublin. Public school: Portora Royal, Enniskillen; excellent academic and sporting record.

1923–7 Trinity College, Dublin, first as pensioner, then as foundation scholar. In BA examinations placed first in first class in Modern Literature (French and Italian); awarded large gold medal and Moderatorship prize. Active in Modern Languages Society, Cricket Club, Golf Club; keen chess player. Summer 1926: first contact with France (bicycle tour of the châteaux of the Loire).

1928 Spends first two terms teaching at Campbell College, Belfast.

1928–30 Exchange *Lecteur* at Ecole Normale Supérieure in Paris, almost contemporaneously with Jean-Paul Sartre. Meets James Joyce. Summer 1930: Beckett's first separately published work, the poem WHORO-SCOPE, issued by Nancy Cunard's Hours Press in Paris.

1930–2 Assistant Lecturer in French, Trinity College, Dublin. Resigns after four terms. 19–21 February

1931: performance of Beckett's first dramatic work, LE KID, a parody sketch after Corneille written in collaboration with Georges Pelorson, French *Lecteur* at Trinity.

1931   PROUST, his first and last major piece of literary criticism, published by Chatto and Windus.

1932-7   *Wanderjahre* culminating in the decision to settle permanently in Paris.

1933   Death of his father, who leaves him an annuity which forms the bulk of his slender income until the royalties from GODOT twenty years later.

1934   Chatto and Windus publish MORE PRICKS THAN KICKS (short stories).

1935   ECHO'S BONES AND OTHER PRECIPITATES (first collection of verse) published in Paris.

1938   MURPHY, his first novel, published by Routledge. An Oxford undergraduate, Iris Murdoch, deeply influenced by the book.

1942   Resistance group in which Beckett is active is betrayed to the Gestapo; he escapes to the unoccupied southern zone with only minutes to spare.

1942-4   Ekes out a living as an agricultural labourer not far from Avignon ('. . . we were there together, I could swear to it! Picking grapes . . .', WAITING FOR GODOT, p. 62). Writes WATT, his last English novel.

1944-6   Returns to Ireland to see his family, then in order to get back to France, accepts a post as interpreter and storekeeper at the Irish Red Cross hospital in Saint-Lô (Normandy).

1946-50   Back in Paris, burst of creative activity. Writes in French the essential works of the canon, the trilogy of novels (MOLLOY, MALONE DIES, THE UNNAMABLE) and the play WAITING FOR GODOT, which was preceded by ELEUTHÉRIA.

1950 Mother dies.

1951 MOLLOY and MALONE DIES published in Paris ('getting known . . .', *Krapp's Last Tape*, p. 17).

1952 WAITING FOR GODOT published in Paris.

1953 World première of WAITING FOR GODOT in Paris, 5 January, director Roger Blin.

1954 Beckett's English translation of GODOT published in New York.

1955 World première of the English GODOT in London, 3 August.

1957 First broadcast of ALL THAT FALL by BBC (13 January), director Donald McWhinnie. Creation of ENDGAME (French text, with ACT WITHOUT WORDS I) in London, 3 April, director Roger Blin.

1958 World première of KRAPP'S LAST TAPE in London, 28 October, director Donald McWhinnie.

1959 Hon. D.Litt., Dublin University. EMBERS wins Italia Prize.

1961 World première of HAPPY DAYS in New York, 17 September, director Alan Schneider. International Publishers' Prize, shared with Borges.

1962 First broadcast of WORDS AND MUSIC by BBC (13 November).

1963 Creation of PLAY (in German translation) at Ulm, 14 June, director Deryk Mendel. First broadcast of CASCANDO by RTF, 13 October, director Roger Blin.

1964 FILM made in New York, director Alan Schneider.

1965 Creation of COME AND GO (in German translation) in Berlin, September, director Deryk Mendel.

1966 EH JOE televised by BBC (4 July), production by Michael Bakewell.

1969 Nobel Prize for Literature. First independent production of BREATH (originally incorporated by Kenneth Tynan as the opening sketch in OH! CALCUTTA), Glasgow, October, director Geoffrey Gilham.

I

Introduction

In the popular imagination Samuel Beckett conjures up tramps, dustbins and prolonged inactivity. To the commentators – and seldom can a writer within twenty years of his first success have given rise to such a formidable heap of interpretation – he is the occasion, like the forest of Arden to the banished Duke in *As You Like It*, for 'tongues in trees, books in the running brooks, sermons in stones'. The irony inherent in this double view of him must have given Beckett – more of a lover of the joke for its own sake than perhaps either the popular or the academic party will allow – much quiet pleasure. All the same, the two views, that there is nothing to Beckett beyond dustbins and that there is everything conceivable beyond dustbins, quite clearly suggest, taken together, the nature of his dramatic method. What I hope to show here is that the Beckettian demonstration is a thoroughly dramatic one; that, in other words, though he set out as poet and novelist and was quoted quite recently as seeing himself as a novelist who also writes plays, the point at which his public found him and he found his public was the right one. Samuel Beckett was waiting for the theatre as the theatre was waiting for Samuel Beckett.

Camillo's Memory Theatre

Although it would be unwise to try to pull together in a few pages the history of the theatre, it is necessary, before closing in on Beckett's theatre, to have some idea of its context, if only so as not to confuse it with literature. And since Beckett himself is in many ways the last heir to the Renaissance, an heir who has religiously devoted himself to selling off every last stick and stone of his inheritance, it is appropriate to begin with an illustration drawn from the Renaissance. In Chapter Six of *The Art of Memory*, Frances A. Yates describes 'The Memory Theatre of Giulio Camillo'. This amazing contraption was built in Venice and visited, in 1532, by a friend of Erasmus in the company of its inventor. The spectator stood on the stage before an auditorium divided into seven grades and seven gangways and intended to contain the sum of wisdom and knowledge, classified according to the stages of creation and the planetary gods, and furnished with an elaborate system of 'memory images' drawn from classical mythology, under each of which were placed drawers or boxes filled with written material relating to the 'memory image'. 'It begins', as Dr Yates says, 'to look like a highly ornamental filing cabinet. But this is to lose sight of the grandeur of the Idea – the Idea of a memory organically geared to the universe.' Erasmus' friend described his visit to Camillo's Memory Theatre as follows:

> He calls this theatre of his by many names, saying now that it is a built or constructed mind and soul, and now that it is a windowed one. He pretends that all things that the human mind can conceive and which we cannot see with the corporeal eye, after being collected together by diligent meditation may be expressed by certain corporeal signs in such a way that the beholder may at once perceive with his eyes everything that is otherwise hidden in the depths of the human mind. And it is because of this corporeal looking that he calls it a theatre.

Apart from giving us a remarkably clear view of the Renaissance frame of mind, the belief that it is possible to know and do everything (a belief which Beckett turns precisely on its head), Camillo's Memory Theatre helps us to see, in pictorial terms, the nature of the theatrical experience; what happens when actors are on a stage and people watching them. Imagine first that behind the 'spectator' on the stage, instead of a back wall, the theatre opens out into a second auditorium, the exact replica of the first, but this time filled with an audience: the 'spectator' contemplates the sum of wisdom and knowledge gathered in Camillo's auditorium, while the audience in the second auditorium contemplates the 'spectator'. Now give the 'spectator' speech, gesture, movement, so that he can express, for the benefit of the audience, what he discovers, or is reminded of, in Camillo's auditorium; give him also, if necessary, assistant 'spectators', as well as props, scenery, sound and lighting effects. Now shut off or remove Camillo's auditorium, which corresponds, for our illustration, with the period of preparation of a theatrical event, the work of the playwright, director and actors in rehearsal; and let the 'spectators', now become actors, repeat on successive nights the particular selection from the sum of wisdom and knowledge which they have prepared.

The curious point is this: that while the event on the stage is a more or less ossified, drastically reduced piece of Camillo's grand 'mind and soul', the audience itself, taken together in all its variety of character and individual experience, is a kind of living, breathing sum of wisdom and knowledge; and the excitement and uniqueness of the event, each night, consists in the reaction set up between the selected, ossified, classified and the collected, amorphous, unclassified. In other words, the real theatrical dialogue is that between the 'mind and soul' of the audience and its image on the stage, while the exchange of words between actors is merely one means among many of expressing or perhaps 'fishing for' that other dialogue, which is, of course, never exactly the same two nights running.

This somewhat idealised audience, a compendium of wisdom and knowledge, as prompt to display its riches as

Camillo's filing cabinet, would evidently require playwrights and actors of similar stamp, demi-gods preferably, of translucent and at the same time highly developed personality, for whom every possible experience would be of equal importance and viewed with equal equanimity. But audiences naturally share the outlook of their time and place, with all that implies of narrowed sight, prejudice and almost unconsciously bounded thought. They are apt to arrive at a theatre not only with strong preconceptions about life outside the theatre, but also of how that life can be most fittingly discussed in the dialogue between stage and auditorium. They arrive, that is to say, in a dual capacity, partly as participants in the dialogue, partly as arbiters of the content and form of the dialogue.

The knowledge that this is so has a direct effect on the playwright and actors, who must decide either to conduct the dialogue within the limits expected by the audience or to attempt to extend those limits, whether of form or content, or both. The first course leads to a more amicable dialogue between themselves and the audience, but is in danger as time goes on of leading to diminishing returns, of becoming a habit, of degenerating from a live dialogue into a set of dead responses. The playwright is the first to lose by this development, since the actor can, by virtuoso performance, sustain a dialogue with the audience long after the horse he rode in on has died under him; but even when the actor has succumbed in his turn, the audience loses little or nothing, for it simply abandons all interest in a dialogue with the stage, arrives for the third act, ogles and gossips during the interval, looks forward to dinner, and generally parcels out amongst itself all the animation it shared in days gone by with the stage.

For actors, then, and even more for playwrights, the better course is the second; and certainly nearly all those playwrights one can still name, from Aeschylus who introduced the second actor, to Beckett who introduced the waiting as a guiding principle, have chosen it; have chosen, that is, not simply to conduct a limpid meeting of minds with the audience, but to lock horns and tussle with it over the what or the how, or both the what and the how. One can hardly overestimate the effect this has on the nature of the dialogue between stage and audience, on the nature of the theatrical experience. Why did Chekhov, who now seems so 'lifelike', so 'true', so 'moving', and all the rest of it to huge, appreciative audiences, once seem 'boring', 'trivial', 'depressing' to all but a few? Surely because then the dialogue between him and his audience was suffused with challenge on his part and angry reaction on theirs; it was not that the audience which was against him then was 'wrong', any more than the audience which is for him now is 'right'. The quality of the dialogue has changed with the removal of a particular colour from it, rather as the appearance of paintings changes by the effect of time.

So that when considering Beckett's work we have to take into account not only the strong presence of this 'colour' in his dialogue with the audience, but also, only seventeen years after his dialogue began, the beginnings of its disappearance. Whether he likes it or not, the Nobel Beckett (his own dig at Yeats) is no longer the same Beckett, for the purposes of the theatrical experience, as the one castigated by an enraged member of the audience in his unpublished and unperformed first play, *Eleuthéria*: 'Beckett, Samuel, Béquet, Béquet, he must be a Greenland Jew crossed with an Auvergnat.'

But even when this top 'colour' has disappeared, when a play has ceased to be 'provocative'or 'controversial' in the most superficial sense, the dialogue between stage and audience continues to be a kind of struggle: the events on the stage and the interpretation given them by those on the stage are subject at every moment to re-interpretation by the audience, so that the performance advances by a continuous series of readjustments. And whereas in the more or less amicable dialogue of, say, a farce or Shaftesbury Avenue comedy, these readjustments are limited to a few surprise developments within a predictable story and no readjustment whatever is necessary for the manner of telling the story (since the audience already knows as well as those on the stage how such a story is told), they can become, in the hands of a master of the art, whether playwright, actor or director, a relentless and heroic wrestling-match, like that between Odysseus and Proteus, in which the Proteus on the stage will not give up the story he knows until the Odysseus in the auditorium has seized and held him through every conceivable change of shape.

It follows from this that a play is not a simulation of life outside, any more than football is, or the circus, or a game of chess, but an activity in itself, neither less nor more real than any other activity; its artificiality consists only in the fact that it is deliberately condensed to fit a particular time and place, and that the terms of the struggle are in some measure prepared in advance. The answer to Hamlet's question 'What's Hecuba to him, or he to Hecuba' is that they are parties to a theatrical dialogue, in which, though Hecuba may not be the real Hecuba of history, she is the present occasion for real emotion in him and he the occasion for her occasioning it.

All the theatrical upheavals of the last hundred years or so, the frenzied theorizing, experiment, internal warfare between one faction and another have been directly caused by the desire on the part of those working in the theatre to reappraise, sharpen and extend beyond existing limits this vital encounter with the audience. For although it is often supposed that when an art becomes interested in itself it is growing narcissistic and losing contact with 'life', the truth is that these periods of introspection betray not self-satisfaction but the reverse, a sense of the inadequacy in making contact of the methods previously practised; and that what one might at first take to be a barren obsession with form for its own sake is actually the search for an improved, more living language. Just as the object of continually refining the design of the horseless carriage or the early aeroplane was to obtain better performance, so the repeated attempts at formal innovation in the theatre have been directed at obtaining more reality, not less.

But it is important not to confuse this reality, the reality of the theatrical experience, with 'naturalism', which is only one of the forms, though perhaps the most insidious and ingratiating, used to obtain reality. Naturalism aspires, by imitating as closely as possible the surface appearance of life outside the theatre, by judicious selection and well-placed hints, to awaken fresh perceptions in its audience; as, for instance, by placing the scene of the rich man in his castle immediately after the scene of the poor man at his gate, to give the audience a new view of that well-worn relationship, but in such a way that life itself seems to have written and directed the play. The obvious advantage of naturalism is the ease with which an audience can grasp its convention, seeing reality inside the theatre just as they are accustomed to seeing it outside; and the life of this particular theatrical dialogue consists in the extra intensity with which they can be brought to see it. The disadvantages, however, are grave. In the first place, the illusion may make itself too strongly felt: the smell of the poor man's plate of soup, the trappings of the rich man's castle, may monopolize the audience's attention, turning what set out to be a dialogue into no more than the display and reciprocal admiration of a charming doll's house. In the second place, even if the illusion is kept sufficiently within bounds, those on the stage are constantly compelled to subordinate their encounter with the audience to their imitation of life, pretending the audience is not there, pretending the actors have never met before, never heard each other's lines before, discreetly concealing wads of essential information under everyday conversation, like spies at a café table. In the theatre (as opposed to the cinema or television where it is perhaps the natural form) naturalism is clumsy, in that it has to heave mountains in order to bring forth mice: it is an example of form outgrowing content.

The alternative to naturalism (a form which conveys the illusion of being made by nature) is an overtly man-made, artificial form: as specific to the theatre, as inexpressible in other terms as that of painting or music. This is the form envisaged by Edward Gordon Craig in his essay *On the Art of the Theatre:* '. . . The Art of the Theatre is neither acting nor the play, it is not scene nor dance, but it consists of all the elements of which these things are composed.' It is the same form, though judged now more from the point of view of its effect on the audience, that hovers luridly in front of Artaud: 'Everything that acts is a cruelty. It is upon this idea of extreme action, pushed to its limits, that the theatre must be built.' Apollinaire searches for it in his surrealist play *The Breasts of Tiresias* and illustrates very clearly what he is after in the preface to his published text:

> In order to attempt, if not a renovation of the theatre, at least an original attempt, I thought it necessary to come back to nature itself, but without copying it photographically. When a man wanted to imitate walking he created the wheel, which does not resemble a leg. In the same way he has created sur-realism. . . .

The Russian director Meyerhold calls it 'the stylized theatre' which 'produces a play in such a way that the spectator is compelled to employ his imagination *creatively* in order *to fill in* those details suggested by the stage action'.

The problem for the artist using such a form is twofold: first, to perfect a theatrical language (not simply speech, but the whole experience as it emanates from the stage) which not only expresses his particular subject-matter, but is inseparable from it, so that what an audience is seeing at every moment is not, for instance, a tree, but a tree seen by Chekhov, or a tree seen by the actress Olga Knipper, or a tree seen by the director Stanislavsky, or best of all a tree seen by all three at the same time; secondly, to have an audience grasp the conventions of that language sufficiently to take part as avidly as possible in the dialogue, without, on the other hand, grasping them so easily and completely that it becomes bored and switches on the automatic pilot of habit. The dialogue between stage and audience lives on the constant tension between opaqueness and transparency, and if the tendency of the nineteenth-century popular theatre and its successors in our own day has been to melt into unalleviated transparency, the besetting sin of the innovators of the last hundred years or so has been to overdo the opaque, to forget the existence of the leg in their excitement over the wheel, to substitute expressionism for expression. And this surely accounts for the extraordinary persistence of naturalism, which besides being a clumsy method on the stage is also unsatisfying to an audience in that its concentration on illusion and imitation allows so little scope for the imagination: an audience would still rather be unsatisfied than turned to stone in its seats by total incomprehension.

But however difficult it may be to obtain, however rarely it has in practice been achieved, what the theatrical innovators have been trying to create is quite simply an artificial experience which is self-sufficient, as natural experiences are self-sufficient; and as natural objects are unique, autonomous, their 'subject-matter' being inseparable from their form, so that we cannot say that a blade of grass, an insect or even a man is 'about' anything, in the same way the work of art, the play, is to be perceived and enjoyed through its unique shape, the crystallization of its 'subject-matter'. 'For Proust', Beckett has written, 'the quality of language is more important than any system of ethics or aesthetics. Indeed he makes no attempt to dissociate form from content. The one is a concretion of the other, the revelation of a world' (*Proust*,

p. 88). It is this concretion and revelation, this two-way shape, the shape made and the shape perceived, which constitutes a theatrical experience of the kind I have suggested. In his earliest published work, an essay on Joyce's *Work in Progress*, we find the twenty-three-year-old Beckett passionately resorting to italics in his urge to communicate this basic article of his artistic creed:

> Here form *is* content, content *is* form. You complain that this stuff is not written in English. It is not written at all. It is not to be read – or rather it is not only to be read. It is to be looked at and listened to. His writing is not *about* something; *it is that something itself.* ('Dante . . . Bruno . Vico . . Joyce.')

The theatre, an act of 'corporeal signs', 'a built or constructed mind and soul', as Camillo's Memory Theatre reminds us, was waiting for the forty-six-year-old Beckett to make good his words.

Mr Endon's Game of Chess

Waiting for Godot, first performed in 1953, was written in 1948, the same year as and immediately after Beckett's novel *Molloy* and its sequel *Malone Dies*. The third part of this trilogy of novels, *The Unnamable*, was written the next year. During the last four years of the 1940s, the first four years of his forties, Beckett wrote, in French, all the work which can now be seen clearly as the central portion of his artistic achievement, including as well as the four works already mentioned the aborted novel *Mercier et Camier* (1946), four short stories (1946), the unpublished play *Eleuthéria* (1947), the *Three Dialogues with Georges Duthuit* (1949) and the thirteen *Texts for Nothing* (1950). In an interview with Israel Shenker in 1956, Beckett had this to say:

> I wrote all my work very fast – between 1946 and 1950. Since then I haven't written anything. Or at least nothing that has

seemed to me valid. The French work brought me to the point where I felt I was saying the same thing over and over again. For some authors writing gets easier the more they write. For me it gets more and more difficult. For me the area of possibilities gets smaller and smaller. . . . At the end of my work there's nothing but dust – the nameable. In the last book – *L'Innommable* – there's complete disintegration. No 'I', no 'have', no 'being'. No nominative, no accusative, no verb. There's no way to go on. The very last thing I wrote – *Textes pour Rien* – was an attempt to get out of the attitude of disintegration, but it failed.

Before taking up this point in discussing Beckett's development during and after the four central years, it is necessary to go back on his tracks up to and including 1948, the year of *Molloy* and *Waiting for Godot*. Bearing in mind a remark of Beckett's: 'I conceived *Molloy* and what followed the day I realized my own stupidity. Then I set myself to write about what I feel', let us follow the advice offered in another: 'If you want to find the origins of *Waiting for Godot*, look at *Murphy*.'

The eponymous hero of Beckett's first novel, written in 1935, does not, on the face of it, seem to be the direct ancestor of any of the characters in *Waiting for Godot*. He is evidently the direct ancestor of the heroes of Beckett's other *novels*, Watt, Molloy, Malone and the rest, as he is equally evidently the descendant (in a literary sense) of Belacqua, the hero of Beckett's first book of stories, *More Pricks Than Kicks*, written in 1933. He is distantly related, of course, to Vladimir and Estragon, in *Waiting for Godot*, but only via Molloy and the two heroes of the aborted novel *Mercier et Camier*. Similarly, the other chief characters in *Murphy*, two Irish academics and two Irish temptresses, share only the most vestigial characteristics with Pozzo and Lucky: they move on set courses with frantic animation, like clockwork toys, as Pozzo does, while the contents of Lucky's mind would not surprise them, even if his garbled delivery would. They are, however, clearly present in the stories that make up *More Pricks Than Kicks* and less clearly, translated from Anglo-Irish types to French bourgeois types, in the unperformed play *Eleuthéria*, of which Belacqua, alias Murphy, alias Victor is again the hero. The essential difference between Murphy and the other characters in his novel is stated unequivocally: 'All the puppets in this book whinge sooner or later, except Murphy, who is not a puppet.'

Just as Belacqua's stories are located in Dublin, which Beckett finally left in 1932, Murphy's story unfolds between Dublin and London, but for the most part in London, where Beckett lived between 1933 and 1936. In other words, Belacqua and Murphy, whatever their wishes in the matter, are firmly lodged in time and place, just as Victor, the hero of the play *Eleuthéria*, is even more reluctantly aware that he lives in Paris. Belacqua drives off for his second honeymoon in a borrowed Morgan, Murphy visits Lombard Street in ostensible search of a job, a friend of Victor's parents tries unsuccessfully to give him a ride in a Delage. The trappings of an active consumer society boldly assert themselves and all these heroes can do is turn away their eyes, seek solitude in public bars like Belacqua, retire to a rocking-chair or the Cockpit in Hyde Park like Murphy, or stay in bed like Victor. In *Waiting for Godot*, the boot is on the other foot: the trappings have become derisory relics belonging exclusively to Pozzo – his half-hunter watch, his pipe, his camp-stool, his picnic-hamper, his vaporizer – all of which he has lost before the second Act.

Nor are the dynamics of *Murphy* at all like those of *Waiting for Godot*, being based on the principle of pursuit and escape, Murphy escaping and the 'puppets' pursuing either him or each other. *Waiting for Godot* functions by ebb and flow, anticipating the behaviour of the light and temperature in Beckett's novel-on-a-pinhead *Imagination Dead Imagine*, published in 1965: 'Such variations of rise and fall, combining in countless rhythms, commonly attend the passage from white and heat to black and cold, and vice versa' (*No's Knife*, p. 162). *Murphy*, by contrast, is much more reminiscent of Racine's *Andromache* as Beckett is reported to have pictured it during his brief spell as a lecturer at Trinity College Dublin, in 1931: 'The characters in *Andromache* are shown chasing each other round the circumference of a circle.'

The most noticeable thing about *Murphy* is its manner. Although ostensibly a comic novel, containing many sustained comic passages as well as incidental shafts of wit, its third-person narration betrays a kind of nervous arrogance, a distaste amounting almost to disdain for its 'puppets' which is always on the edge of being a contempt for its readers, who may be assumed to be more like the 'puppets' than the non-puppet, Murphy. Murphy, in other words, who is presented as being only interested in burying himself in himself and letting 'the big world' go hang in favour of 'the little', his own consciousness, is actually asserting his superiority to the reader in this respect more than either he or his narrator will let on. The humorous sallies are apt to contain an element of one-upmanship, the suggestion that if you do not see the joke, it is against you.

This manner is common to all Beckett's early work. Belacqua, the hero of *More Pricks Than Kicks*, may owe his name and his view of himself to Dante's Belacqua, from Canto IV of the *Purgatorio*, who because of his laziness when alive was sitting out the whole length of his life again in Ante-Purgatory among the late-Repentant before being admitted to Purgatory proper; but Beckett's Belacqua is certainly due for a long spell among the intellectual snobs even after he has purged himself of his indolence. Indeed, his indolence is not true indolence at all, being far too carefully organised, it is much more a matter of Belacqua being too intelligent for this world and its piddling activities and therefore preferring to play a game according to his own rules which will at the same time call in question the rules generally in vogue. Beckett's first poem, *Whoroscope*, which won him ten pounds in a competition in 1930, is one long intellectual 'dare', stuffed with recondite incidents from the life of Descartes, which Beckett was reading at the time, furnished with only partially helpful notes in the manner of Eliot's *The Waste Land*, and written in an elliptical and queasily hearty style after Browning and again Eliot. And this arrogance is even more marked in the early critical works, the essay on Joyce's *Work in Progress* and the study of *Proust* which, although a table of the law for any student of either Proust or Beckett, is, to say the least, dictated from a great height.

It would be pointless to pick at that particular fault in a young and ambitious writer which is common to nearly all ambitious young writers, were it not that we have here, in the negative, a key to the origin of *Waiting for Godot*, or rather of '*Molloy* and what followed'. Beckett has never been one to make statements about himself and his work lightly, and when he says 'I conceived *Molloy* and what followed the day I realized my own stupidity' he is not being politely deprecating, he is telling us precisely what happened. One day, perhaps in March, perhaps at the end of a jetty in a howling wind (see Chapter 6), he discovered that there was something false about his early work, that his heroes' professed desire to lose at the game of life was bogus, that they actually wanted to win and were sneakily using all their considerable intellectual ability, mordant wit and accumulated reading to prove the world wrong so as to prove themselves right. From that moment he took such a dislike to his heroes, at least to their pretensions and evasions, to their reflection of himself, their author (that carefully groomed heir to the Renaissance), that he dropped most of his previous rancour towards 'the big world' and concentrated on pulling to pieces, straw by straw, his own and his heroes' view of it.

This gave rise to a changed relation between Beckett the author and his characters. The characters, ceasing to have his approval, ceased trying to escape from 'the big world' and began failing to escape from him. Instead of beginning from him, the intellectual, the possessor of so much knowledge, the gifted writer, and aiming somewhat dishonestly, or at least unsuccessfully, to be nothing, they began from the nothing he now saw them as and had no aim at all; while he, the writer, separated from them now as he never had been before, pursued them like a ruthless sleuth, pinpointing and shortly afterwards removing from them every last 'something', every pretension that still stood in their way to being nothing. In *Murphy* the narration was in the third person, as it was in *More Pricks Than Kicks* and even in *Watt*, written in 1942 (the narrator being actually named Sam). In *Molloy* and the stories (collected in *No's Knife*) which immediately precede and lead into *Molloy*, the narration is in the first-person: a clear indication of the characters' new independence from their author, since he now allows them to behave and speak in their own person, instead of constantly nudging them and elucidating them in his.

The difference between Beckett's early heroes and his mature ones is actually figured in *Murphy* and prefigured in *More Pricks Than Kicks*, in the story called *Walking Out*. Belacqua, descending 'one fateful fine Spring evening' from a walk in the hills near Dublin with his 'Kerry Blue bitch' and reaching the road, sees 'an old high-wheeled cart, hung with rags'. 'Squatting under the cart a complete down-and-out was very busy with something or other. . . . Belacqua took in the whole outfit at a glance and felt, the wretched bourgeois, a paroxysm of shame for his capon belly.' But the Kerry Blue bitch pees on the man's trousers, just as Belacqua draws level with the cart:

> 'Good evening,' he piped in fear and trembling, 'lovely evening.'

A smile proof against all adversity transformed the sad face
of the man under the cart. He was most handsome with his thick,
if unkempt, black hair and moustache.

'Game ball,' he said.

After that further comment was impossible. The question of
apology or compensation simply did not arise. The instinctive
nobility of this splendid creature for whom private life, his joys
and chagrins at evening under the cart, was not acquired, as
Belacqua one day if he were lucky might acquire his, but antecedent, disarmed all the pot-hooks and hangers of civility.
Belacqua made an inarticulate flourish with his stick and passed
down the road out of the life of this tinker, this real man at last.
(*More Pricks Than Kicks*, p. 112)

The self-defensive humour of the rest of the book is for
once almost abandoned in this passage, leaving the romanticism of words like 'nobility' and 'splendid' quite unguarded,
undenied, but it is the word 'antecedent' which has most to
say. Belacqua, Murphy, and Beckett in them can never have
this 'antecedent' private life, they can only aim to acquire it,
but what Beckett realized when he found Molloy was that he
could give his characters 'antecedent' private lives if he could
relieve them of the burden of himself, Samuel Beckett, the
educated, the self-consciously artificial man.

Murphy's noble tinker is a man called Mr Endon, an in-
mate of the Magdalen Mental Mercyseat, the asylum in the
outskirts of London where Murphy becomes a male nurse.

It seemed to Murphy that he was bound to Mr Endon . . . by
a love of the purest possible kind, exempt from the big world's
precocious ejaculations of thought, word and deed. They
remained to one another, even when most profoundly one in
spirit, as it seemed to Murphy, Mr Murphy and Mr Endon.
(p. 127)

Mr Endon, then, not only has an 'antecedent private life'
but he makes Murphy feel that he has one too, an improvement on Belacqua's tinker. Mr Endon is a schizophrenic

whose 'one frivolity' is playing chess, and it is the game of chess he plays with Murphy, during Murphy's single tour of night-duty in the corridors of the Magdalen Mental Mercyseat, which I take to be if not the pure and simple origin of *Waiting for Godot*, certainly the clearest illustration of what Beckett meant when he drew attention to *Murphy*.

Beckett calls the game 'An Endon's Affence', suggesting in his loftily cryptic manner that its principle is on the lines of 'defence is the best form of attack'. Anyone may play the game through for himself, since the author is thoughtful enough to lay out all the moves in two columns (pp. 165–7) and to provide besides a set of drily humorous notes which are considerably more helpful than those attached to his poem *Whoroscope*. Mr Endon plays Black, and his 'Affence' develops as follows: his two Knights hop over the curtain of black pawns and make, as it were, their opening bow, while his King's Rook does a single little chassis all to itself in its corner; by the end of Mr Endon's eighth move all three pieces are back in their places and it is as if Mr Endon had never begun. After that, having displaced the two central pawns and thus opened the curtain, Mr Endon puts his two Rooks, two Knights, two Bishops, King and Queen through a gracefully symmetrical dance among themselves, the whole performance being conducted with impressive gravity, except that after the thirtieth move the King and one of the Rooks stand on their heads. At the end of the dance, on what would be the forty-fourth move, if Murphy did not surrender on the forty-third, Mr Endon's pieces are all back where they started, except for the two pawns in the middle, which being pawns cannot retreat.

Murphy's game all this while has been little short of despicable. Starting with the classic opening which Beckett identifies in a note as 'the primary cause of all White's subsequent difficulties' (p. 167), Murphy divides his moves disastrously between exact copies of Mr Endon's and initiatives of his own. At his twenty-seventh move, with what a note describes as 'the ingenuity of despair', Murphy puts his Queen directly in front of Mr Endon's curtain of pawns, moves her along in front of them temptingly at the next move. Mr Endon's pawns are unmoved. At his thirty-second move, Murphy's King sets out sturdily for the front line, and at the thirty-fourth Mr Endon's Queen, in the natural course of her stately gavotte, puts Murphy's exposed King in check, though Mr Endon says never a word. His status insultingly reduced by this neglect Murphy's King begins to commute feebly between two equally insignificant squares, until after a final 'abject offensive' with one of his Knights Murphy surrenders, leaving his own pieces scattered at random all over the board.

The first thing to be said is that the game could not have followed the course it did, if Murphy had not admired Mr Endon so much, considered him the only 'real man' he had ever met, desired so passionately to be like him. The second thing is that Mr Endon makes his moves strictly in accordance with the rules of chess, with the difference only that he is not playing with the aim of defeating his opponent but of returning to his exact starting-point. The third thing is that in spite of having no end in view except his beginning, Mr Endon clearly enjoys the rhythms, patterns, shapes of the interim. The fourth thing is that although Mr Endon doesn't rationally need Murphy – he could have danced his dance equally well without a White piece on the board – it is nevertheless he who set up the pieces, issued the silent invitation, and that he therefore derives some secret satisfaction from having Murphy play with him, though his only recognition of Murphy's presence is that he lets him start and plays in turn.

We can see, then, that Mr Endon's game of chess is Mr Beckett's game of writing. He is Murphy, wishes to be Endon, but cannot because being neither mad nor a tinker

his private life can only be 'acquired' not 'antecedent'. The
nearest he can get to being Mr Endon is to play with Mr
Endon's Black pieces, obeying the rules of chess, but without
the aim of chess, and enjoying the patterns as he makes them.
He cannot, however, quite do without Murphy, his old self,
because without Murphy there is no sense of Endon, without
his past no measure of his present, without an audience no
performance; and it is the performance of his game of chess
which counts with Mr Endon, as it is the performance of his
game of writing which counts with Mr Beckett, the only
thing which counts: 'The expression that there is nothing to
express, nothing with which to express, nothing from which to
express, no power to express, no desire to express, together
with the obligation to express' (*Duthuit Dialogues*, p. 103).

Beckett still continued in his novels, *Watt*, *Molloy*, *Malone
Dies* and *The Unnamable*, to try to close the gap between
Murphy and Mr Endon. It has often been noticed that Beckett
steadily deprives his heroes of everything they might be
supposed to call theirs: Watt of the normal way of stringing
words together; Molloy of his bicycle and later the use of his
legs; Malone of virtually everything except his rational consciousness of himself; the Unnamable of his 'I', his 'have',
his 'being', his nominative, accusative and verb. This is
usually taken to be either a devastating picture of human
decay or a prolonged philosophical investigation after
Descartes:

> I am, however, a real thing, and really existing; but what
> thing? I have already said it: a thing which thinks. And what
> else? I will stir up my imagination in order to discover if I am
> not something more. I am not this assemblage of limbs called
> the human body; I am not a thin and penetrating air spread
> through all these members; I am not a wind, a breath of air,
> a vapour, or anything at all that I can invent or imagine, since
> I have supposed that all those things were nothing, and yet,
> without changing this supposition, I find I am nevertheless

certain that I am something (Descartes' *Second Meditation*, tr. F. E. Sutcliffe).

Neither view is wrong in itself, but it is necessary to recall that Beckett's books are not social documentaries, nor are they philosophical treatises, they are works of fiction. The pictures of human decay, the appearance of philosophical investigation are metaphors; what Beckett is doing is writing novels and his heroes are writers writing the fiction in which they are embedded, attempting to bring their fiction and themselves as writers to a satisfactory conclusion, to 'say the last word', to rest in the silence from which they began, having made a perfect pattern, like Mr Endon's game of chess, on the way. Of course there are many parallels to be drawn between the act of writing and the act of living, of which it is part, and Beckett exploits such parallels to the full, but whatever the writing of other writers may be, his mature writing is not imitation, it is not, as he said of Joyce '*about* something; *it is that something itself*'.

The transition from *Murphy*, which is still a novel of illusion, an imitation of life, to '*Molloy* and what followed' is made via *Watt*, Beckett's last novel written in English. *Watt* begins firmly in Dublin with a fine comic passage after Beckett's 'old-style', in which a hunchback called Hackett converses with a couple called Mr and Mrs Nixon on a street bench. Watt appears in mysterious circumstances from a tram and the rest of the book is devoted to his adventures. It is made fairly clear that Watt *is* Hackett, a version of Hackett, we may suppose Hackett's fiction of himself, as we may suppose that 'Sam', to whom Watt later relates his adventures in the grounds of some kind of asylum, is yet another version of Hackett. Certainly Sam is less inside the fiction than Watt, he is perhaps even less so than Hackett. The chief part of Watt's adventures takes place in the house of a Mr Knott, where Watt is in service. The house itself is un-

localized, though Watt reaches it and leaves it from a recog-
nizably Irish railway station.

His adventures consist quite simply in getting not to
know himself, in losing his bearings, in moving across the
board from Murphy's comparative sanity (according to the
view of 'the big world') towards Mr Endon's admired in-
sanity, towards his 'antecedent private life'. There are naturally
many echoes of the 'senseless' but beautiful patterns made by
Mr Endon's Black pieces, of which one of the most re-
sounding is the incident of the Galls, father and son, who come
to tune Mr Knott's piano:

> ... Mr Gall Junior brought his work to a close. He re-
> assembled the piano case, put back his tools in their bag, and
> stood up.
> The mice have returned, he said.
> The elder said nothing. Watt wondered if he had heard.
> Nine dampers remain, said the younger, and an equal number
> of hammers.
> Not corresponding, I hope, said the elder.
> In one case, said the younger.
> The elder had nothing to say to this.
> The strings are in flitters, said the younger.
> The elder had nothing to say to this either.
> The piano is doomed, in my opinion, said the younger.
> The piano-tuner also, said the elder.
> The pianist also, said the younger.   (*Watt*, pp. 68–9)

Although we seem to be listening to a conversation between
two of Mr Endon's chess-pieces, a conversation owing something to Lewis Carroll's chess-pieces in *Alice Through the
Looking-Glass*, we are also beginning to hear the dialogue of
Waiting for Godot, certainly to breathe its peculiar atmosphere.
The narrator of *Watt*, who still uses the third person, but in
a way that brings him so close to Watt that it is almost first
person, tells us that the incident of the Galls resembled 'in a
sense' all the incidents in Mr Knott's house:

It resembled them in the sense that it was not ended, when it was past, but continued to unfold, in Watt's head, from beginning to end, over and over again, the complex connexions of its lights and shadows, the passing from silence to sound and from sound to silence, the stillness before the movement and the stillness after, the quickenings and retardings, the approaches and the separations, all the shifting detail of its march and ordinance, according to the irrevocable caprice of its taking place. It resembled them in the vigour with which it developed a purely plastic content, and gradually lost, in the nice processes of its light, its sound, its impacts, and its rhythm, all meaning, even the most literal. (*Watt*, p. 69)

While Beckett went on, in the novels, feeling his way towards Mr Endon, peeling off onion-skin after onion-skin in an attempt to set down the very act of writing, for which, as we have seen, Mr Endon's game of chess was an early metaphor, he turned in *Waiting for Godot* to the chess-board itself. The chess-*players* are absent from the text, though present, one might say, in the author and his audience. Those on the stage are the pieces, and the patterns they make, the shape of their dialogue with the audience 'according to the irrevocable caprice of its taking place', are those made by the Galls, father and son, as perceived by Watt.

Impotence and Ignorance

It would be innocent to suppose that in facing his opponent, the audience, across the chess-board of *Waiting for Godot*, Beckett views it with any more positive goodwill than Mr Endon had for Murphy. A certain tolerance due to its consenting to be there at all, together with a sensitive disdain should it decide not to be there any longer, would be about the sum of his outward manner, as he reveals in a letter to Alan Schneider, apropos of the American production of *Endgame*: 'Success and failure on the public level never mattered much to me, in fact I feel much more at home with the latter,

having breathed deep of its vivifying air all my writing life
up to the last couple of years . . .' Jean-Marie Serreau, director of the Théâtre Babylone, which gave the first performance
of *Waiting for Godot*, describes the rigorous attention Beckett
devoted to rehearsals of *Play*, but adds this curious note:
'Once the thing is finished, in spite of the degree of perfection he demands, Beckett seems to lose interest in it:
characteristically he never attended a performance.' All this is
reminiscent of the younger Beckett who took Proust to task
for certain passages 'when for a space he ceases to be an artist
and raises his voice with the plebs, mob, rabble, canaille'
(*Proust*, pp. 66–7), and who even as recently as 1949 was
dreaming of an art 'too proud for the farce of giving and receiving' (*Duthuit Dialogues*, p. 112). I mention this apparent
incivility of Beckett's only to make clearer the nature of the
theatrical experience he offers. The truth is that it is intended
in the first place to satisfy himself, himself as sole audience,
and that by extension only the member of the audience (as
opposed to the many-headed monster *in toto*) who is willing
to become for the duration of the experience in some measure
its creator can enjoy Beckett's pattern in the way it is intended
to be enjoyed. The words 'satisfy' and 'enjoy' must be understood in a purely aesthetic sense; Beckett's theatre is neither
humane nor friendly, for the simple reason that it is addressed
to himself. There could not be a greater contrast than with the
ingratiating theatre of Bernard Shaw, who addressed, always
and exclusively, other people, in the belief that they needed
guidance and that he had guidance to offer.

The theatrical language of Beckett's plays is that of a man
talking to himself, in the first place the author, and in the
second place each individual member of the audience; and
this 'outer' language between stage and audience extends
also to the 'inner' language of the stage itself, where the
characters too are men or women talking to themselves.
Beckett tells himself a story in the form of a play, each

member of the audience tells himself the story in the form of Beckett's play, and within the play the characters tell themselves stories. What is on the stage is not only the occasion for, the content of the dialogue with the audience, it is also a metaphor, an image of the dialogue between the author and himself as audience, between the member of the audience and himself as author.

In *Waiting for Godot*, two men, usually dressed as tramps, though they might equally well be dressed as Irish literary types (tramps have no monopoly of stinking feet, bad breath, ill-fitting boots, prostate trouble), fill in time on successive evenings on a blasted heath while waiting to keep an appointment with somebody called Godot; on the stage actors fill in time on successive evenings while waiting to go home when the curtain falls; in the auditorium an audience fills in the same time on the same successive evenings while waiting for a dénouement; in his study a little previously the author has filled in time day after day while waiting to complete a play. The three real waitings, those of the author, actors and audience, are brought together in the metaphorical waiting for Godot, and the time that is filled in in the process is the 'shape' of the theatrical experience. Someone who tells us that *Waiting for Godot* is a picture of human life, with elements of a moral or religious tract, is no doubt giving us a perfectly genuine report of his own personal reaction to the 'shape', of the interpretation which for him best bridges the gulf between the uncomposed, natural life he has experienced outside the theatre and the composed, man-made life he has experienced inside it; but he is not telling us what the shape of *Waiting for Godot* itself is.

It is perhaps easiest to conceive of what it is, in terms of painting or sculpture. Matisse's late collages, Mondrian's grids of horizontal and vertical lines, Brancusi's tapered or egg-shaped forms are extractions, essences of experience which can be re-lived by those who see them *directly*, without the intermediary of the natural forms from which they grew. Mondrian's horizontals and verticals do not stand for the horizons and trees of his early landscapes, they are what the horizons and trees were all the time trying to express: the early horizons and trees were standing for the later horizontals and verticals rather than the other way round. Brancusi said: 'Simplicity is not an end in art, but we arrive at simplicity in spite of ourselves, as we approach the true sense of things.' In the same way, Vladimir and Estragon in *Waiting for Godot* are not naturalistic down-and-outs, not cousins of Synge's tinkers, for instance, but whatever it was that Synge's tinkers in Synge's plays, or Belacqua's Syngean tinker in *More Pricks Than Kicks*, were standing for, while Pozzo and Lucky are the 'simplicity', not the simplification of a landowner and his serf. Beckett has said that *Waiting for Godot* is 'a play that is striving all the time to avoid definition' but the very use of the word 'striving' suggests how close the author himself still is to his 'explanations', the explanations that are constantly called for and even frequently supplied in the earlier play *Eleuthéria*. That *Waiting for Godot* was not wholly successful at avoiding definition seems to be confirmed by the brooding reference to it in the fifth *Text for Nothing*: 'Why did Pozzo leave home, he had a castle and retainers. Insidious question, to remind me I'm in the dock' (*No's Knife*, p. 92).

By 1949 Beckett had already begun to take new avoiding action. We have seen how, in the 1956 interview with Israel Shenker, he found 'nothing but dust' at the end of his work and said of the *Texts for Nothing* that it was 'an attempt to get out of the attitude of disintegration, but it failed'. In the *Three Dialogues with Georges Duthuit*, short discussions of the work of three painters, he lays special emphasis on the idea of failure. In the first two Dialogues he attacks the whole notion of artistic achievement, not its value in the past, but its value for the present and future. Painters such as Matisse, he suggests, are not really revolutionaries, they are only disturbing 'a certain order on the plane of the feasible' (p. 103). In the third Dialogue, apropros of the Dutch painter Bram van Velde, Beckett rebukes Mondrian ('No painting is more replete than Mondrian's,' p. 124) and goes on to claim that the relation between a painter's subject and his means, his 'manner of dispatch', has been dogged by an increasing sense of failure, that the history of painting 'is the history of its attempts to escape from this sense of failure' and that van Velde is 'the first to admit that to be an artist is to fail, as no other dare fail, that failure is his world and the shrink from it desertion, art and craft, good housekeeping, living'. Now whatever one may think of the work of Bram van Velde, whatever one may think of this somewhat too Shavian paradox that a kind of artistic achievement can be judged by its degree of failure, it is nevertheless around the idea of failure, as it were in the search for failure, that Beckett has composed all the plays that follow *Waiting for Godot*.

The idea of failure is of course present in *Waiting for Godot*, in the metaphorical part, notably in Godot's failure to turn up, or the two protagonists' failure to wait for him at the right place, or whatever the reason is for Godot and the protagonists failing to come together, but it is not the princi-ple on which the theatrical experience of *Waiting for Godot* is built. The author, the actors and the audience set out with the intention of filling in time, of waiting for time to pass. Dur-ing the course of the play time has passed, even though as Estragon observes 'It would have passed in any case' (p. 47). Author, audience and actors have kept their appointment: 'We are not saints', says Vladimir, 'but we have kept our appointment' (p. 80). The evening has in this sense been an unalloyed success for all concerned and herein lies the flaw for Beckett. In order to express the failure of his characters, he has resorted to successful means, a successful 'manner of dispatch', whereas for the theatrical experience to be real, at no point illusory, the means also must fail, otherwise it is a play *about* failure instead of an experience of failure.

In the interview with Israel Shenker, after the remarks already quoted, Beckett went on to compare his own work with that of Joyce:

7 NY Times May 6, 1956

> The kind of work I do is one in which I'm not master of my material. The more Joyce knew the more he could. He's tending towards omniscience and omnipotence as an artist. I'm working with impotence, ignorance. I don't think impotence has been exploited in the past. There seems to be a kind of aesthetic axiom that expression is an achievement – must be an achievement. My little exploration is that whole zone of being that has always been set aside by artists as something unuseable – as something by definition incompatible with art. I think anyone nowadays who pays the slightest attention to his own experience finds it the experience of a non-knower, a non-can-er (somebody who cannot).

With the exception of the fragment *From an Abandoned Work*, which was written in 1955 and whose title tells its own tale, Beckett wrote no fiction between 1950 and 1960. He devoted the decade to pursuing failure in two stage-plays, *Endgame* and *Krapp's Last Tape*; two radio plays, *All That Fall* and *Embers*; and two mimes, *Act Without Words I* and *II*. But it is as well to remember, so as not to confuse Beckett's pursuit of failure with the quite separate idea of 'public' failure, that he would almost certainly have written none of these plays if the 'public' success of *Waiting for Godot* had not given him confidence in the theatre.

What he was after now was not simply to create a series of images or pictures of 'impotence, ignorance' on the stage and have the audience, actors and author all at one in waiting for some nebulous issue out of their affliction, as in *Waiting for Godot*; but to leave no loophole, to have all concerned fully aware from start to finish that the experience as a whole – the author's creation, the actors' creation, the audience's participation, as well as the 'story' on the stage – is a web of 'impotence, ignorance'. In this sense Godot himself, in his capacity as a *deus ex machina*, comes to resemble the famous pistol-shot which Chekhov could not do without in his early plays.

But if Mr Endon and Murphy are to be as involved in the failure as their Black and White chess-pieces, they have to be brought on to the board. Vladimir and Estragon accept it as their responsibility to perform improvisations within the time allotted to them by the author, whereas Hamm and Clov, in *Endgame*, are very clearly the authors as well as the actors of their affair, which Clov opens with the uncompromising and unpromising statement: 'Finished, it's finished, nearly finished, it must be nearly finished' (p. 12), so as to leave the audience in no doubt of its complicity in an experience that lacks, as they say, potential. Krapp and his tape-recorder, Henry and his voices in the radio play *Embers*, are at once authors and actors, just as the 'I' characters in Beckett's trilogy of novels are. The two *Acts Without Words* by their nature eliminate the notion of literary authorship, letting their actors appear in the simpler role of authors of their own movements, though the pointedly artificial stage machinery which is used to motivate these movements already prefigures Beckett's next period. Only the radio play *All That Fall* seems to hark back to an earlier period with its feeling of third-person narrative, of an invisible author somewhere above the board controlling a story of impotence and ignorance rather than floundering in the mud of his own failure to know or to be able.

All That Fall excepted, the plays of this period are theatrical images of an author at work, an author 'weary of puny exploits, weary of pretending to be able, of being able, of doing a little better the same old thing, of going a little further along a dreary road' (*Duthuit Dialogues*, p. 103), an author who knows he is doomed to failure even before he has begun, but who continues to try to tell himself stories out of an obscure 'obligation to express'.

Beckett closed the decade and opened a new period in his work with his last full-scale novel, *How It Is*, which, although it is still a fictional image of the author in the act of creation, has undergone a significant change of method. The confessional, diary-like prose of his previous fiction (stylistically indebted to earlier self-confessors such as Augustine, Defoe, Descartes, Sterne) has become a terse and authoritative prose-poetry: 'How it was I quote before Pim with Pim after Pim how it is three parts I say it as I hear it' (p. 7). For all the narrator-hero is swimming in dense tracts of mud throughout, his manner of speaking is as forthright, almost as 'public' as it is clipped. He is still talking about himself, but he has lost his obsession with himself, gained an objectivity which curiously succeeds in bringing the two parts of himself, perceiver and perceived, closer together. And the new clarity with which he views himself seems also to extend to things external to himself: not that the pictorial element was not always strong in Beckett's work, but that it was apt to be misted by half-suppressed, more-than-half-distrusted romanticism. Most significant of all, Beckett now brings his prevailing pictorial element into the foreground so that it takes precedence not only over the story but over the storyteller too. The Unnamable might tell a story about a character called Mahood who lived in a jar, he might even suggest his own surroundings in a fairly vague way, but in *How It Is* one looks for the narrator in the mud, rather than for the mud round the narrator. And just as the diary-prose has become prose-poetry, so the pictorial element has become stylized: mud, as it were, in the abstract.

The tree in *Waiting for Godot*, the bare interior with two small windows and a door in *Endgame*, the 'den' in *Krapp's Last Tape* were all recognizable 'old-style' conventions for natural settings. In the stage-plays that Beckett wrote after

How It Is the pictorial element is predominant and semi-abstract. Winnie, the heroine of *Happy Days* (written in 1961), is buried first to her waist, then to her neck in a mound of scorched grass; the three protagonists of *Play* (written in 1963) are contained in separate urns with only their heads poking out; those of *Come and Go* (written in 1965) are composed on their bench, inside their heavy costumes, under the brims of their hats; the pile of rubbish in *Breath* (first performed in 1969) has either entirely buried its protagonist or expelled him to the wings. The earlier radio plays, *All That Fall* and *Embers*, were both set in detailed natural landscapes, but the two later ones, *Words and Music* (written in 1962) and *Cascando* (written in 1963) have no setting at all, unless it is the studio in which they are performed. On the other hand, the television play *Eh Joe* (written in 1965) and the film scenario *Film* (written in 1964) seem to return to his earlier more naturalistic period. Whenever he makes the test of a new medium, Beckett always seems to take a few steps backward, witness *Waiting for Godot* and *All That Fall*.

The new confidently objective author-subject of *How It Is* dominates the major stage work of this period, *Play*. The theatrical means Beckett has found for expressing him can be traced from the stage machinery of the two *Acts Without Words* through the off-stage bell which marks out Winnie's happy days, but his appearance in *Play* is as perfectly integral to a theatrical experience, as rigorously inseparable from the performance he directs as the narrator of *How It Is* was inseparable from himself as subject of the narration. Stage machinery, bells off-stage or on, however essential they may be to a performance, are not integral, they remain props. But the *sine qua non* of a theatrical event – before sound, scenery, props or characters – is light (or its absence). Light on a stage is the equivalent of print on the page of a novel. The light that flicks on and off the faces of the protagonists of *Play*, corresponding with, eliciting their words, as the darkness corresponds with, elicits their silence, is exactly comparable with the textual layout of *How It Is*, paragraphs of print separated from one another by spaces of blank page. Even the delivery of the speech in *Play* ('Voices toneless . . . Rapid tempo throughout') is the spoken equivalent of the way the novel's text reads.

In *Play* the form is co-existent with the content, for although the light acts as the interrogator of the three protagonists, bidding them speak or be silent by its shining or not shining on each of their faces, it is also the condition of their existence for themselves and for the audience. The metaphor on the stage is the failure of a three-cornered relationship, the staple content of a thousand boulevard comedies (*Play*'s French title is, of course, *Comédie*), but the light in which it is seen, the darkness in which it is not seen are also the author's opening and shutting eye, the actors' prompters and the audience's only means of participation. The 'inner' impotence and ignorance of the metaphor now blend with the 'outer' impotence and ignorance of the means, as the 'inner' and 'outer' waiting blended in *Waiting for Godot*. The two radio plays, *Words and Music* and *Cascando*, written at about the same time as *Play*, use variations of this discovery, adapted to the special circumstances of radio.

Beckett's most recent work in the theatre has not yet gone beyond *Play*, except in paring down the content. In the same way his most recent fiction, the four short pieces, *Imagination Dead Imagine*, *Enough*, *Ping* and *Lessness* (French title: *Sans*), have been parings down of *How It Is*, but it is worth remarking that in these works the pictorial element and the prose-poetry in which it is conveyed are growing still more prominent and concentrated, that Beckett has always in the past used his fiction as the spearhead of changes in his work, and that every new technical impetus in his development has been brought about by the conflict between an apparently pulverized content and Beckett's inexorable 'obligation' to invent a form capable of pulverizing it still further. He has brought his theatre to the threshold of abstraction, but not yet beyond. His dustbins are still self-evidently dustbins and can still give rise to 'sermons in stones', to moral, social and philosophical dissertations, however distasteful he may find them. Whether or not he himself ever makes the final step over the threshold into abstract theatre, whether or not it is possible for the theatrical experience to be genuinely abstract, he has – after the wicked fashion of all outstanding artists – apparently closed every other door in the faces of his successors, just as Joyce must once have seemed to close every door but impotence in his.

'Finished, it's finished, it must be nearly finished.'

—Samuel Beckett, *Endgame*

2

The One That Got Away

ELEUTHÉRIA (1947)

The chief difficulty in discussing an established work of art is that we are apt to be mesmerized by its finished state. The more powerfully *Hamlet* or *Waiting for Godot* assert their existence and the less we are able to conceive of living in a world in which they do not exist, the more impossible it becomes to understand how they were made in a world in which they did not exist and were not even missed, except by the artist himself. Such works often seem as if they had sprung fully grown and fully armed from the head of the artist, like Athena from the head of Zeus after he had complained of a headache, whereas we can hardly doubt that the artist actually laboured and fumbled to make them just as he did to make less successful works. For this reason the value of Beckett's unpublished and unperformed first play as archaeological evidence is enhanced both by its lack of familiarity and by its comparative failure to achieve artistic autonomy.

Although *Eleuthéria* belongs statistically to the group of works Beckett wrote in French after the end of the Second World War (including *Molloy* and *Waiting for Godot*), its stand-offish title – *eleutheria* is the Greek word for freedom – harks back to the poems he published in 1935, whose individual titles (such as *Enueg I* and *II*, *Alba*, *Sanies I* and *II*, *Serena I*, *II* and *III*, and *Da Tagte Es*) seem to hold their subjects out to the reader in self-consciously foreign tongs.

Furthermore, the play's content and characters are, as I have
already suggested, closely related to those of the pre-war prose
works, *More Pricks Than Kicks* and *Murphy*.

Eleuthéria is set in Paris, on 'three successive winter after-
noons', and concerns the family Krap, M and Mme Henri
Krap and their son Victor, together with various friends,
relations and dependants. In form it is a straightforward
bourgeois comedy in three Acts, except that for the first two
Acts Beckett divides the stage in two. In the first Act the
'principal' action takes place in the Krap family's salon, while
the 'marginal' action, silent but for a single phrase and confined chiefly to desultory movements on Victor's part, takes
place in Victor's bed-sitting-room elsewhere in Paris. Victor
is thus 'present at his own absence', as Beckett once described Proust's Narrator paying an unexpected call on his
grandmother (*Proust*, p. 27). In the second Act Victor's bed-
sitting-room, viewed from another angle, becomes the scene
of the 'principal' action, while the 'marginal' action, con-
sisting again of a single phrase and a few movements, is
placed in the Kraps' salon. In the third Act the bed-sitting-room
viewed from yet a third angle, fills the stage, the Kraps'
salon having, in the words of Beckett's own note at the head
of the play, 'been pushed into the pit by the shift of scene'.

This crude technical device, of putting two scenes on stage
at once in order to achieve a contrapuntal action, almost
always turns out to be disastrous in practice. The reason is, I
think, that human bodies moving about on a raised platform
are only prevented from appearing too large and clumsy by
most careful attention to proportion, and that the awkward
effect made on the eye by a vertical splitting of the proscenium
rectangle – the emphasis this places on the sheer size of the
human figures – obliterates whatever subtleties the contrapuntal action may offer to the intelligence. Beckett did
not attempt to use the device so overtly again, though we can
find its traces in *Waiting for Godot* in the division between

Vladimir and Estragon on the one hand and Pozzo and Lucky on the other, as well as in *Endgame*, in the division between Hamm and Clov on the one hand and Nell and Nagg on the other. The divisions in these plays are built into the whole theatrical effect and express the barrier between two sealed-off views of the world far more clearly than a mere splitting of the stage area. In *Krapp's Last Tape* the device has become so sophisticated, so perfectly integral to the theatrical experience (the dialogue of a man with his past self, expressed through a single actor and his own tape-recorded voice) that we should perhaps not recognize it at all, but for the similarity of the protagonists' names.

The action of *Eleuthéria* is simple enough. The Krap family have lost contact with their son Victor, who has de-liberately withdrawn, after the manner of Murphy and pre-viously Belacqua in *More Pricks Than Kicks*, from what the narrator in *Murphy* calls 'the big world's precocious ejacula-tions of thought, word and deed' (*Murphy*, p. 127). The first Act observes the Kraps and their friends and relations at their ejaculations, the second Act observes their attempts to bring Victor back to the fold and the third Act brings the audience in on the side of the Kraps in a final effort to ex-tract from Victor if not a recantation at least an explanation of his conduct, or lack of conduct. The chief bully-boys in the various assaults on Victor's freedom change from Act to Act. Mme Krap having failed to persuade him in the first Act, her friend Mme Meck (*mec* in French means 'pimp'), feebly assisted by a hired thug and her chauffeur, makes an abortive attempt to kidnap him in the second Act. Explana-tions are demanded of Victor by a glazier, commonsense representative of the man-in-the-street, who is present ostensibly for the purpose of mending a broken window-pane in Victor's room. This glazier, incidentally, has an assistant-cum-son; not only is their relationship similar to that of Moran and his son in the second part of *Molloy*, and to that of the Galls, father and son, in *Watt*, but the conversation between them at the end of Act Two of *Eleuthéria* is plainly a model for Vladimir's conversations with Godot's messengers at the end of each Act of *Waiting for Godot*. The glazier, however, is no more successful at browbeating Victor than Moran will be at tracking Molloy, and it is left to a supposed member of the audience, descending from his box on to the stage, to extract – with the help of a Chinese torturer – a satisfactory confession from the victim.

In the light of Mr Endon's game of chess, this member of the audience's own explanation of why he has not already left the theatre is sufficiently remarkable:

> No, if I am still here, it is because there is something about this affair which literally paralyses me, strikes me dumb. How can I explain this to you? Do you play chess? No. Never mind. It's like watching a game of chess between two tenth rate players. Three quarters of an hour have gone by and neither of them has touched a piece. There they are like two half-wits gaping at the board; and there you are, even more half-wit than they, riveted to the spot, nauseated, bored to extinction, worn out, flabbergasted by such stupidity. Finally you can't stand it any longer. You say to them: 'But for God's sake do this, do this, what are you waiting for, do this and it's finished, we can go off to bed.' There's no excuse for you, it's against all the rules of good manners, you don't even know the blokes, but you can't help yourself, it's either that or hysterics.
>
> (*Eleuthéria*, p. 103)

After this lively description of one of Beckett's later plays in action, Victor's confession sounds somewhat etiolated:

> I have always wanted to be free. I don't know why. I don't even know what that means, to be free. You might tear my nails out by the roots and still I couldn't tell you. But far beyond words I know what it is. I have always wanted it. I still want it. I want nothing else. First I was the prisoner of others. So I left them. Then I was the prisoner of myself. That was worse. So I left myself.   (*Eleuthéria*, p. 115)

Beckett's difficulty here – the difficulty for all playwrights and especially those who start as novelists – has been to manage without the covering of prose narration. Having been able, in *More Pricks Than Kicks* and *Murphy*, more or less to conceal under an ironic narration the essentially adolescent mawkishness of both Belacqua and Murphy, he finds nothing for poor Victor to stand up in. No wonder that Victor is at such pains throughout the play to avoid explanations, to avoid, indeed, all speech and action so far as possible. Not only is he likely to seem to an audience, if he ever appeared in front of one, the most pallid protagonist ever to occupy a stage, he evidently seems so even to his creator. This is the nub. There is a vast difference between a character who is intended by his author to be 'pallid' according to rules previously observed in the creation of characters and a character in whom the author himself fails to distinguish any colour. The final stage direction – 'Then he lies down, his thin back turned on humanity' – must fail of its effect for the simple reason that a faceless character has no back to turn. Beckett never again makes the elementary mistake of using a protagonist whose one desire is to escape from himself without giving him a self to escape from.

The prototype of Beckett's later heroes is really Victor's father, Henri Krap, though even he, in achieving death at the end of the first Act, is given his ticket of leave with rather too generous a hand. Henri is that staple element of *bourgeois* comedies, the skeleton at the feast. His role is to sit in the midst of his wife's salon taking the stuffing out of everyone else's enjoyment, or pretence at enjoyment – a role which he performs with engaging relish:

> I am the cow which, at the gates of the slaughterhouse, realises all the absurdity of pastures. A pity she didn't think of it sooner, back there in the long lush grass. Ah well. She still has the yard to cross. No one can take that away from her.
>
> (*Eleuthéria*, p. 13)

Henri's first name reappears on the hero of *Embers*, his second name and some of his manner on Krapp, and his modest talent as a *poseur* is ably improved upon by Hamm in *Endgame*, but his particular line in dry wit at the expense of other people's effusions brings him closest perhaps to Mr Rooney in *All That Fall*. Not that Henri Krap has it quite all his own way. The rest of the cast may correspond schematically to the 'puppets' in *Murphy*, being there simply to illustrate 'all the absurdity of pastures', but just as the young Beckett in *More Pricks Than Kicks* revealed a certain aptitude for portraying the antics of social gatherers, so the denizens of Mme Krap's salon can't help entertaining while they illustrate. The atmosphere is one peculiar to the less smooth reaches of the middle class, an atmosphere of mild perturbation and half-suppressed fidgets. The servants are too few and too thick-witted, the room is no doubt badly ventilated and all the characters are probably suffering from dyspepsia. They also have an instinctive urge to assert their own individuality, however insignificant – composed as it is mainly of a few assorted off-the-peg characteristics which scarcely add up to a 'character' – so that their manners tend to be abrupt, verging from time to time on the openly rude. 'You look like death,' says Mme Krap's sister, Mme Piouk, as she disengages herself from her sister's embrace and sits down. 'You don't look very lively yourself,' retorts Mme Krap quick as a flash. Mme Piouk's husband, the well-named Dr Piouk, is himself a serious rival to Henri Krap as chief *épateur des bourgeois*. After refusing to drink or smoke, Dr Piouk lights a cigarette. 'I thought you didn't smoke,' says Henri. 'I lied,' says Dr Piouk.

Now this excursion into the salon, which may at first thought seem a place alien to Beckett, is actually basic to most of his later plays, far more so than his appearance on the open road in *Waiting for Godot*. Pozzo comes hot from such a salon (even if with Irish furniture) as his need to be asked to sit down testifies. Nell and Nagg may be physically confined in dustbins, but their hearts are in their own salon; Hamm and Clov still live in theirs, though somewhat decayed. Henry in *Embers*, Joe in *Eh Joe* have salons in their background; the three characters in *Play* have two salons in theirs; while as for Winnie in *Happy Days* and the three women in *Come and Go*, they are surely only developed versions of Mme Krap, Mme Piouk and Mme Meck. Mme Krap even speaks of Mme Meck as though she were Winnie: 'Jeanne sees life and gaiety everywhere. It's a permanent delusion.' Only Krapp seems to have moved spiritually into something more like Victor's bed-sitting-room.

This is an important point since it serves to remind us that Beckett's characters are shaped by middle-class backgrounds, that whatever their present settings may suggest to the outward eye, in the matter of dustbins, mounds of scorched earth or funerary urns, the characters still see themselves surrounded by the 'elegant circular table, four period chairs, armchair, standard-lamp and shaded wall-light' of the Kraps' salon. These are, in other words, domestic, interior plays, belonging to the main tradition of European domestic comedy, and it is from this tradition that they fetch the rhythms of their dialogue, their frame of reference and very often their phraseology, that 'dead language', as Mr Rooney calls it, with which they struggle so picturesquely. Beckett's theatre, as he himself once remarked, is most at home behind a proscenium arch.

This in its turn has a particular effect on the relations of the characters to one another. They are not, like the characters in Greek tragedy, in many of Shakespeare's plays, or in Brecht's, the mere visible tip of an iceberg, whose invisible part is a whole population, any of whom might at any moment put in an appearance; rather the stage on which they are set, the interior which encloses them, is their whole world; they are locked in as in Sartre's play *Huis Clos*. There is no one beyond themselves, they are stuck with one another, Vladimir with Estragon and both with Pozzo and Lucky; Hamm with Clov and both with Nell and Nagg; Krapp with his past selves; Henry with his voices; Winnie with Willie and so on. In *Eleuthéria* this atmosphere of total enclosure is still largely unconscious, as it is in most of the domestic comedies from which *Eleuthéria* descends, but already in *Waiting for Godot* it has become a major conscious element of the drama (Godot himself being the forlorn hope of escaping it) and in all the later plays it exercises a centripetal force.

Victor's sense of freedom from others and from himself, however inadequate its expression, is precisely what Beckett the playwright withholds from every other character in the canon, and the dramatic tension which Victor so easily snaps by being allowed to turn his back on the whole affair from the beginning is never slackened again. Every one of Beckett's mature characters would follow Victor's recipe for escaping from himself if he could:

> By being as little as possible. By not stirring, not thinking, not dreaming, not speaking, not listening, not perceiving, not knowing, not wanting, not being able, and so forth. It seemed to me that those were my prisons. (*Eleuthéria*, p. 116)

The point is that while passionately desiring to escape, not one of them can. There lies the scene.

3

Bailing Out the Silence

WAITING FOR GODOT (1948–9)

One evening, on a lonely country road near a tree, two elderly men, half-tramp half-clown, are waiting for someone of the name of Godot who has, they believe, given them to understand that their patience at the rendezvous will be rewarded. The two, Estragon ('Gogo') and Vladimir ('Didi'), are not sure what form Godot's gratitude will take, any more than they know for certain whether they have come to the right place on the appointed day. They occupy the time as best they can until distraction arrives in the shape of Pozzo, a local landowner on his way to the fair to sell his slave Lucky. Pozzo halts awhile with Estragon and Vladimir, eats his lunch in their presence, even grants them his bones when his menial spurns them, and then in gratitude for their society has Lucky dance and then think aloud for them. The three become so agitated by Lucky's intellectual performance that they all set upon him and silence him. Not long afterwards Pozzo takes his leave, driving Lucky before him. Estragon and Vladimir have not been alone many moments together before a small boy appears with the news that Mr Godot 'won't come this evening but surely tomorrow'. The boy departs, night falls abruptly, and after briefly contemplating suicide by hanging themselves from the tree, the two men decide to call it a day, but despite their decision to go, do not move as the curtain falls.

The curtain rises the next day on a scene identical except

for the fact that the tree has sprouted a few leaves. Vladimir is joined on stage by Estragon and much the same things happen, except that when Pozzo and Lucky appear (from the side they made their exit from in Act One), Pozzo turns out to have gone blind and Lucky dumb. After all four collapse on top of each other and then somehow manage to get up again, Pozzo becomes exasperated at Vladimir's questions about time, bellowing that life itself is only a brief instant. He leaves, driving Lucky before him, from the side he had entered from in Act One. After another brief interval the boy comes on a second time and delivers the same message as before. The sun sets, the moon rises abruptly, the two men again contemplate suicide, but without much determination, and then, despite their agreement to leave, make no movement as the curtain falls. So ends the play in which, as one critic wittily but inaccurately put it, nothing happens, twice.

Perhaps the most striking thing about Beckett's second work for the stage is its maturity. This impression springs mainly from the fact that it is a convincingly created dramatic image, that the dialogue is ably constructed and the characterization effectively conceived. It is to some extent a misleading impression, however, since the text now available was established only after a number of versions had been tried out. The original French manuscript is still unpublished, but enough is known about it to show that it was a rather hesitant piece of work: Beckett was not sure what names to give his characters, for instance, and even whether or not to make Godot a real presence in the action by suggesting, for instance, that Estragon and Vladimir have a written assignation with him, or that Pozzo himself is Godot failing to recognize those he has come to meet. These matters were settled in the first French edition which preceded Roger Blin's creation by a few months, but even this text differs in certain respects from the second, post-performance edition. In production, moreover, Blin advised certain cuts for reasons of technical effectiveness, and at that stage in his dramatic career Beckett was only too ready to learn from a professional. When he undertook the first English translation, therefore, he dropped most of the passages Blin leaves out, and then, in the definitive edition of 1965, not only seized the opportunity of restoring the Lord Chamberlain's censored passages, but also of making a large number of minor amendments to the dialogue and directions which considerably enhance the play's theatrical effectiveness. So that the text we now possess has gone through a considerable polishing process in manuscript and in print, both on the stage and off it. When we recall that this development has taken place over a period of some fifteen years, the transition from the jettisoned *Eleuthéria* is not as abrupt as might at first sight appear. Although the first draft of *Godot* was written quickly, in a matter of just over three months, the way had been prepared for it by *Eleuthéria* as well as other Beckett works. We have noted that the model for Vladimir's exchanges with Godot's boy-messenger lay in the glazier's conversations in the earlier play; detailed analyses have revealed close similarities between the novel *Mercier et Camier* and *Waiting for Godot*; and as we saw in the Introduction, Beckett himself has said that the play's origins may be sought in *Murphy*.

Of course, *Waiting for Godot* also has its antecedents within the broader context of the post-naturalist tradition. A few of the analogues that have been cited are Strindberg's *Dream Play*, with its sense of repetitiveness and unreality, Synge's *The Well of the Saints*, Jarry's *Ubu* cycle (Pozzo is distinctly ubuesque), Vitrac's *Victor or The Children Take Over*, not to mention the classic Chaplin who developed his astonishing persona after observing the gait of a drunken cabby. And Beckett is close, naturally, to another great poet of inertia, Chekhov. Their plays share a feeling of inconclusiveness: apart from the sale of the estate, for example, nothing much can be said to happen in *The Cherry Orchard*. The heroine goes back to her unsatisfactory lover in Paris, other characters turn again to their idle dreams, and the proposal of marriage which Varia had been hoping Lopahin would make her does not materialize. Frustrations and a sense of impotence felt by many of the characters provoke tensions between them, and lead to the occasional eruption which subsides as suddenly as similar explosions of anger between Vladimir and Estragon. A forced gaiety in most of Chekhov's characters masks an awareness of abandonment and hopelessness experienced by them; none the less, like Beckett's, they continue to hope unrealistically for a better world just over the hill. Both dramatists excel in laying bare both the nature of life without real hope of improvement or change, and the subterfuges we adopt to conceal from ourselves the worst facts about our condition, in dialogue that modulates with striking rapidity from the sublime to the ridiculous, speech without consequence reflecting action without conclusion. In spite of all, indeed, both Chekhov and Beckett offer us a subdued form of comedy to illustrate Nell's profound dictum in *Endgame*: 'Nothing is funnier than unhappiness . . . It's the most comical thing in the world' (p. 20), since to laugh at our misery is the only way we have found of coming to terms with it. *Waiting for Godot* shows parallels, too, with some of Yeats's plays. In *The Cat and the Moon* of 1926, for example, two beggars, one halt and the other sightless, have for years managed to compensate their respective infirmities by the blind man carrying the lame man on his back. But these and others are largely fortuitous congruences, facts of theatre history to be accorded no more than their due, which is to reveal that *Waiting for Godot* does not stand in splendid isolation.

In several ways, indeed, it is a somewhat traditional play. As spectators we are, for example, launched directly into the action, *in medias res*, and the relatively few details we need for comprehension of the past career of the characters are filled in for us as we go along. Vladimir's 'So there you are again' (p. 9), assumes a previous history of association between himself and Estragon which the spectator, perfectly normally, takes on trust. The time-scale, too, is clearly theatrical rather than actual. When Vladimir, only a few minutes in real time after his entry in Act Two, says of Lucky's hat, 'I've been here an hour and never saw it' (p. 71), Beckett is using one of the oldest dramaturgical tricks for suggesting greater duration than has in fact elapsed.

It is often said that the new forms of drama which arose in the nineteen-fifties, and of which *Waiting for Godot* is so outstandingly representative, flout all the rules of traditional dramaturgy. To an extent this is true enough; but it is also a fact that more recent developments, particularly in the field of improvisatory drama and the happening, have outstripped the earlier avant-garde, revealing how even in its anti-rhetoric it still preserved rhetoric, and how zealously it maintained the hallowed distinction between stage and auditorium. I shall have more to say about the rhetoric of *Godot* later; but the sense of being in a theatre, *qua* theatre, is certainly something the play relies upon implicitly. Just imagine what would happen if a member of the audience took it into his head to cross the footlights and join in the delicately orchestrated banter between the characters! The effect would be the same as on the notorious occasion when an outraged spectator felt impelled to warn Othello against the machinations of Iago. The existential divide between the two worlds of actors and theatregoers is even, in this play, dwelt on with coy jocularity. With his gesture of gazing into the wings, 'his hand screening his eyes' (p. 13), Estragon is being absurdly theatrical, as he is also in his unflatteringly ironic comment about 'inspiring prospects' when looking the audience pointedly in the eyes a little later. Vladimir situates one of the local landmarks, a bog, in the auditorium, and

comically sympathizes with Estragon's hesitation in Act Two
to take cover by running in that direction, despite the fact
that 'there's not a soul in sight' (p. 74). Pozzo in particular
shows an old pro's awareness of where he should be: 'It
isn't by any chance the place known as the Board?' he asks
in Act Two (p. 86). The play's perfect sense of theatre can
thus be explained partly in terms of its self-conscious awareness of theatre.

But it is also attributable in part to Beckett's fine ear for
eminently actable dialogue, once the problem of the frequent
occurrence of virtually identical cues has been overcome in
rehearsal. The vividly conjugal bickering of Vladimir and
Estragon is a case in point. Vladimir is the anxious type, and
Estragon shows few scruples about needling him where he is
most vulnerable. 'What are you insinuating,' Vladimir asks
in some alarm, 'that we've come to the wrong place?' (p. 14),
as Estragon proceeds to undermine his confidence. His
companion continues mercilessly insidious in his questions:
'But what Saturday? And is it Saturday? Is it not rather
Sunday? Or Monday? Or Friday?' He soon tires of this,
however, and leaves Vladimir with his cruel dilemma about
whether they have turned up on the right day and at the right
place for their appointment with Godot. He is impatient in a
general way with Vladimir's restlessness, his habit of waking
him from his cat-naps, his slowness in grasping points of
logic ('Use your intelligence, can't you?' he barks when
Vladimir fails to see why the heavier of the two should be
the first to attempt suicide by hanging from a dubious branch).
On a more brutal level, Pozzo torments Lucky with a calculatedly sadistic brand of boorishness and feigned com-
miseration. As for the language Estragon and Vladimir use
when addressing Pozzo, this varies from the timorously
respectful in the first Act to the familiarly condescending in
the second. In every case the language shows a pithy accu-
racy and liveliness, with a touch of Dublinese ('get up till I

embrace you' is a typical Irishism), but otherwise lacking in distracting provincialisms: a universal form of English speech that is characteristic of Beckett's international background and of the fact that his play was conceived in a perfectly fluent French before it was recast in the author's mother tongue.

The dialogue none the less shows certain features which are characteristic of Beckett's manner as we have come to know it through increasing familiarity with the style of his prose written both for armchair reading and for stage performance. One of these verbal tics is the device of cancellation or qualification, which seems to stem from a deep-seated scepticism about the medium of language itself. Molloy, for instance, says of a man he has been observing, 'A little dog followed him, a pomeranian I think, but I don't think so' (*Three Novels*, p. 12), without showing himself in the least perturbed by the *volte-face*. Similarly with Vladimir, who twice qualifies his admission of ignorance about the nature of the tree: 'I don't know,' he asserts, adding at once, 'A willow' (pp. 14, 93). An analogous hesitation perhaps explains why some of the play's many questions, which make up twenty-four per cent of all utterances according to Barry Smith, terminate in a full-stop rather than a question-mark, so that it is hardly surprising that replies account for only twelve per cent of all remarks. But questions diffidently put are one thing; questions long held in suspense, like 'We're not tied?' (p. 19), or not answered at all, such as 'Like to finish it?' (p. 21), are another thing altogether. Estragon, for instance, is promised an account of 'the time Lucky refused' by Pozzo, who has said enigmatically and menacingly 'He refused once' (p. 40), but the hope of further information on this score, as on others, is cheated. Much of the dialogue, in fact, simulates the inconsequential spontaneity of everyday speech, in which the different participants tend to pursue a line of thought independently of each other – a technique

which Harold Pinter, in particular, has raised to the level of
high art. Beckett counterpoints resulting misunderstandings
with comic subtlety, as in this exchange, which precedes
Lucky's speech:

POZZO. Gentlemen, you have been . . . civil to me.

ESTRAGON. Not at all.

VLADIMIR. What an idea!

POZZO. Yes yes, you have been correct. So that I ask myself is
there anything I can do in my turn for these honest fellows
who are having such a dull, dull time.

ESTRAGON. Even ten francs would be welcome.

VLADIMIR. We are not beggars!

POZZO. Is there anything I can do, that's what I ask myself, to
cheer them up? I have given them bones, I have talked to
them about this and that, I have explained the twilight, ad-
mittedly. But is it enough, that's what tortures me, is it
enough?

ESTRAGON. Even five.

VLADIMIR. That's enough!

ESTRAGON. I couldn't accept less.

POZZO. Is it enough? No doubt. But I am liberal. It's my nature.
This evening. So much the worse for me. For I shall suffer,
no doubt about that. What do you prefer? Shall we have him
dance, or sing, or recite, or think, or –

ESTRAGON. Who?

POZZO. Who! You know how to think, you two?

VLADIMIR. He thinks?

POZZO. Certainly. Aloud.   (*Waiting for Godot*, p. 39)

Such comic misunderstandings are pure vaudeville: 'I must
have thrown them away. – When? – I don't know. – Why? –
I don't know why I don't know?' (p. 67), is another typical
example. But even here the language is rooted in common
speech, in which time is lost through confusions over the
precise meaning of words. 'Are you friends?' blind Pozzo
asks in Act Two, provoking Estragon to noisy laughter: 'He
wants to know if we are friends!' Vladimir mediates here as

on other occasions by pointing out, 'No, he means friends of
his' (p. 85). The dialogue owes a great deal in fact to the
classic stichomythia of music-hall cross-talk routines, in which
a 'straight' man is placed opposite a 'funny' man who de-
lights the audience by becoming embroiled in the complexities
of some problem his partner is attempting, with diminishing
patience, to elucidate for his benefit. In this play, as we have
seen, Estragon tries to explain to Vladimir that since he is
the heavier of the two he should logically try hanging himself from the bough first: 'if it hangs you it'll hang anything',
he concludes with some exasperation (p. 18). The comedy of
this is reinforced when the initial premise itself is brought
into question: 'But am I heavier than you?' asks Vladimir,
who is usually cast as a thin and nervous man opposite
Estragon's stouter and more turgid physique. Another well-
worn music-hall gag is mirrored repetition: both Estragon
and Vladimir, for example, almost simultaneously shake and
feel about inside a favourite object, Vladimir his hat, and
Estragon his boot (pp. 10–11), and both men exclaim his-
trionically 'Hurts! He wants to know if it hurts!' within a
minute of each other (p. 10). This last joke follows the pattern
of so many rhetorical appeals to the audience of the following
type: 'Thin? I'd say my wife is thin. When she swallowed a
pickled onion whole, the neighbours started talking' (quoted
by Benny Green in *Radio Times*, 23 April 1970). Estragon is
equally knowing in this characteristic piece of cross-talk:

ESTRAGON. And we?
VLADIMIR. I beg your pardon?
ESTRAGON. I said, And we?
VLADIMIR. I don't understand.
ESTRAGON. Where do we come in?
VLADIMIR. Come in?
ESTRAGON. Take your time.   (*Waiting for Godot*, p. 19)

Another form of music-hall comedy was the monologue,

which Dan Leno and Arthur English made their speciality: in this play it is Pozzo who practises the art, in his disquisition on the twilight which terminates gloomily, 'That's how it is on this bitch of an earth' (p. 38), as well as – of course more sombrely – in his tirade in Act Two about life taking up but an instant as 'they give birth astride of a grave' (p. 89). But Vladimir too has his set-pieces, for instance the comic banter which begins, 'Let us not waste our time in idle discourse!' and proceeds to do just that (pp. 79–80).

The circus is another source of *Godot*'s unique brand of humour. Anouilh likened the play to the *Thoughts* of Pascal performed as a comedy sketch for clowns. Certainly the totters, the pratfalls, the tumbles, Estragon's trouser-dropping, Vladimir's duck-waddle, Lucky's palsy and Pozzo's cracking of his ringmaster's whip are all lifted straight from the repertoire of the big top. The amount of gesture in a play reputedly actionless is in fact extraordinary. Estragon and Vladimir, for instance, entertain themselves and their audience at one moment by swapping hats in a complex routine which leaves Vladimir significantly in possession of Lucky's, the source of the menial's eloquence. The hats themselves are a direct tribute to the masters of silent-film comedy, Chaplin and Keaton, and their talkie successors Laurel and Hardy. All of this (music-hall patter, circus clowning and movie costume) is taken, even down to the round song and the lullaby which Vladimir offers us, from the most popular and unpretentious forms of entertainment, where what is lacking in subtlety and finesse is made up for in well-drilled smoothness and in perfection of timing. Like such cruder art forms, this play must be well paced if it is to succeed: the bursts of action or of verbal ping-pong must really move, and the indicated silences which punctuate them must be genuinely palpable halts. If this is done, the play's characteristic rhythm comes forcibly across, and reveals not only the wit, but also the sheer entertainment that resides in a work unjustly thought of as gloomy and boring. How can a play like this be dull, if Estragon's priceless howler (in asking a question answered pages before, p. 41) is delivered as it should be, with an old trouper's exact sense of timing? Or if Pozzo's words and actions are exploited as they should be, by an actor with the requisite presence and physique which the role cries out for? Far from weakening or trivializing the work, a director who brings its comic elements out accurately enables the play's serious meditation on the vanity of human wishes to be made all the more forcibly.

The vital thing for any production of this play to achieve, in fact, is a proper tautness. It may not be constructed along traditional lines, with exposition, development, peripeteia and dénouement, but it *has* a firm structure, albeit of a different kind, a structure based on repetition, the return of leitmotifs, and on the exact balancing of variable elements, and it is this structure which must be brought out in production. The sort of repetition the audience must be conditioned to respond to can be seen in the following example. Pozzo, having eaten his meal and lit his pipe, says with evident satisfaction, 'Ah! That's better' (p. 26). Two pages later Estragon makes precisely the same comment, having just gnawed the remaining flesh off Pozzo's discarded chicken bones. But the circumstances, though similar, are not identical: Pozzo has fed to satiety, Estragon has made a meagre repast of his leavings. The repetition of the words in different mouths is therefore an ironical device for pointing a contrast, like that between Pozzo's selfish bellow 'Coat!' to Lucky in Act One, and Vladimir's selfless spreading of *his* coat round Estragon's shoulders in Act Two.

The entire movement of the play, therefore, depends on balance. 'It is the shape that matters' Beckett once remarked apropos of the Augustinian saying which underlies so much of the play's symbolism: 'Do not despair – one of the thieves was saved; do not presume – one of the thieves was damned.'

It is certainly the shape that matters here: the director must bring out the 'stylized movement' which Beckett himself stressed in discussion with Charles Marowitz, a movement which relies heavily on asymmetry, or repetition-with-a-difference. In both Acts, for instance, Pozzo's arrival is curiously foreshadowed by one of the men imagining he hears sounds of people approaching; and whereas in the first Act the two prop Lucky up, in the second they serve as 'caryatids' to Pozzo. But the most poignant example is the ending of the two sections, where the wording is identical, the punctuation varied only slightly to slow down delivery the second time, but the roles reversed: in Act One Estragon asks the question, but Act Two gives it to Vladimir:

VLADIMIR. Well? Shall we go?
ESTRAGON. Yes, let's go.

The first time round, these two sentences can be delivered at more or less normal speed, but on the second occasion they should be drawn out, with three- to six-second pauses between their constituent phrases. When this is done, the intense emotion generated in the auditorium as the last curtain falls is redolent of great sadness.

But the asymmetrical reproduction of nearly everything in two Acts of unequal length is not the only structural feature in the play. Another is the manner in which the counterpointing of the Act-structure is mirrored in the contrasted characterization. Estragon's name is composed of the same number of letters as Vladimir's; the same applies to Pozzo and Lucky. Hence they find themselves associated, and have been joined in a complex sado-masochistic relationship for many years. But their natures obviously conflict: Vladimir is the neurotic intellectual type, Estragon the placid intuitive sort; Pozzo is the bullying extravert, Lucky the timorous introvert. Vladimir instinctively sympathizes with Lucky, and for Pozzo Estragon experiences a degree of fellow-feeling. Vladimir and Pozzo, like Lucky and Estragon who kick each other, are at the extremes of the poised poles. Estragon is afraid of being 'tied', Lucky is tied in effect; Vladimir kow-tows to authority, Pozzo asserts it forcibly. The characters, in fact, like the occurrences both major and minor, are held in uneasy equilibrium within this play.

Yet another of its structural features is the way the writing modulates continually from one tone to its opposite. Pozzo's declamation on the night, for instance, shifts almost violently from the false sublime to the prosaically ridiculous, and after rising to 'vibrant' heights lapses to 'gloomy' depths, and ultimately to inevitable silence. After a long pause, Estragon and Vladimir strike up and swap vaudeville remarks:

ESTRAGON. So long as one knows.
VLADIMIR. One can bide one's time.
ESTRAGON. One knows what to expect.
VLADIMIR. No further need to worry.
ESTRAGON. Simply wait.
VLADIMIR. We're used to it. (*Waiting for Godot*, p. 38)

The transition is masterly, almost musical in subtlety, like the sound of the strings when the brass dies away. Similar modulation occurs between the high jinks of the business around Lucky in Act One and the high grief of Vladimir's cross-examination of the Boy in Act Two, culminating in the great cry from the mass, 'Christ have mercy on us!' (p. 92). Farce and pathos are closely mingled throughout, but perhaps most obviously at the start of Act Two in the clowns' loving embrace which ends, appropriately, in a grotesque pratfall.

The whole of Act Two, in fact, shows a slightly different tone from Act One. The cross-talk is of a more 'intellectual' and less overtly music-hall kind; the confident Pozzo of the first Act is changed into the sightless decrepit of Act Two; and the words of the Boy, delivered 'in a rush' in Act One, have to be dragged out of him by Vladimir the second time

round. The entire second panel of this diptych is less naturalistic, and assumes familiarity with the two down-and-outs
and their ways which permits a briefer restatement of the
theme. Pozzo enters later, and is sooner gone. Lucky's
monologue of Act One, despite its repetitious and garbled
jargon, made a point: that man, notwithstanding the existence of a caring God of sorts and progress of various kinds,
is in full decline; even this statement from a degraded man of
reason cannot recur in Act Two, because, we learn with
terror, he has gone dumb.

Lucky's speech, however, like so much else in the play, is
calculatedly deceptive if we expect it to yield a significant
key to the work as a whole. Those who are perplexed by the
play's 'meaning' may draw at least some comfort from the
author's assurance that it means what it says, neither more nor
less. It is perhaps easier to accept this, now that his other
works are better known; easier indeed than fifteen years ago,
when it was not so evident that Beckett is no didactic writer
concerned to put across a 'message' in dramatic form. Even
the many Christian echoes in the play must now be seen to
add up not to any coherent religious statement, but rather
to a meditation upon a world governed by no other divinity
than some sort of malignant fate; a world in which man waits
and hopes for something to give value to his life and dis-
tract him from the absurdity of his death. 'For there comes the
hour,' Malone writes, 'when nothing more can happen and
nobody more can come and all is ended but the waiting that
knows itself in vain' (*Three Novels*, p. 242). It is a diffuse
awareness of this which informs the bickering, the histrionics
and the horseplay of *Waiting for Godot*, a meditative rhapsody
on the nullity of human attainment written for performance
by an ever-hopeful troupe of circus clowns, bailing out the
silence from a sinking ship of a play which is Beckett's
magnificently rebellious gesture to an art-form he then proceeds to disrupt and transcend.

4

Son of Oedipus

ENDGAME (1954–6)

Beatrice, Lady Glenavy, in her book of memoirs called *Today We Will Only Gossip*, mentions several members of Beckett's family in Dublin whom she had come to know through Beckett's aunt Cissie. Cissie Beckett was at one time an art-student with Lady Glenavy and later married William Sinclair, of whom Lady Glenavy writes:

> For some reason or other he was always known as 'The Boss'. It is hard to describe Cissie's husband except by saying he was a very 'colourful personality'. He had a certain amount of natural charm but he tried to invest himself with an outsize Walt Whitman-like quality. The result of this was more comic than impressive. He was a better person when he was just being himself.

It would be misleading to suggest that 'The Boss' was precisely Pozzo, that the 'outsize Walt Whitman-like quality' with which he tried to invest himself passed directly into Hamm, but in discussing a play as densely made as *Endgame*, which Beckett himself has called 'more difficult and elliptical, relying as it does chiefly on the power of the text to carry one along, more inhuman than *Godot*', it is perhaps worth recalling that this author has been no more immune to everyday experience than anyone else. At any rate Lady Glenavy was not much baffled by *Endgame*:

> After 'The Boss' died, his wife Cissie slowly became crippled with arthritis. I used to go to see her in her house by the sea at Rahevy where she lived with some of her family. She often

spoke of her nephew Sam Beckett with great affection, and when he came from Paris to see his mother at Foxrock he went to visit Cissie also. He would take her for a drive or a turn in her wheel-chair along the sea-road. She used to say with pleasure, 'Sam was here' or 'Sam is coming'.

When I read *Endgame* I recognised Cissie in Hamm. The play was full of allusions to things in her life, even the old telescope which Tom Casement had given me and I had passed on to her to amuse herself with by watching ships in Dublin Bay or sea-birds feeding on the sands when the tide was out. She used to make jokes about her tragic condition, she once asked me to 'straighten up the statue' – she was leaning sideways in her chair and her arthritis had made her body heavy and hard and stiff like marble. As I did what was asked I saw tears of laughter in her eyes. Cissie finished her days in a rather dreary home for old people. I gathered from her that Sam still came to see her and that his visits brought her much happiness.

There is no key to *Endgame* any more than there is to Beckett's own life or to the life of anyone else. Rather there is a mass of detail lodged together, whose general effect is likely to seem different to every comer simply because every comer will naturally pick out some details at the expense of others. We have learnt by now not to look for a specific meaning in a piece of music or a painting, but perhaps because the theatre tends to be a conservative art it is still widely believed to be a branch of the post-office, intended primarily for conveying messages. *Endgame* is not the first play to counter this belief, but it is possibly the first to make a deliberate point of countering it:

HAMM. We're not beginning to . . . to . . . mean something?
CLOV. Mean something! You and I, mean something! (*Brief laugh.*) Ah that's a good one!
HAMM. I wonder. (*Pause.*) Imagine if a rational being came back to earth, wouldn't he be liable to get ideas into his head if he observed us long enough. (*Voice of rational being.*) Ah, good,

now I see what it is, yes, now I understand what they're at!
(*Endgame*, p. 27)

But there being no key does not mean that the play is vague or that it does not have a strong personality of its own. Its personality is all the stronger since we have not come across it before: *Endgame* is an entirely artificial experience and in its totality unique. If we wished to describe the experience of *Endgame* as a whole we would have to say that it was *Endgame* and nothing else at all. The details are another matter. In these we can find resemblances, recognitions, resonances whether from life outside the theatre, like Lady Glenavy, or from previous works of art (including Beckett's own). The mistake would be to suppose that we had contained any part of the play in these receptacles or had done anything but assist ourselves towards being thoroughly immersed in the unique experience of *Endgame*.

In the third Act of *Eleuthéria* it transpires that the hero, Victor, whose apparently motiveless withdrawal from 'the big world' is the motive force of the play, has confessed himself privately, off stage, to his father's valet, Jacques. This character, who if *Eleuthéria* were ever to be performed would certainly have to be played by an actor suitable for the part of Clov, finds himself quite unable to express what Victor told him, whereupon the Glazier, the 'rational being' in this play, loses his *sangfroid*:

JACQUES. It was clear at the time. It's not something one can repeat. It's rather like music.
GLAZIER. Music! (*He comes and goes in front of the door.*) How many crimes in thy name! (*He stops.*) Music! Oh, I see what you mean. Life, death, freedom, and all the rest of it, and the little twisted smiles to show one isn't taken in by the big words, and the profound silences, and the palsied gestures to imply that it isn't that, ho no, that's what one says, but it isn't that, it's something else, something completely different, only to be expected, words are not made to express

such things. So silence please, at least that decency, goodnight
all and happy dreams, we were mad but it's over, mad to dare
speak of anything higher than the price of margarine. Oh
I can hear it from here, your music. You were all tight
naturally.   (*Eleuthéria*, p. 97)

One is likely to feel some sympathy with the Glazier's point
of view in that *Eleuthéria* does fall back on the 'little twisted
smiles . . . the profound silences and the palsied gestures'
for the reason he suggests. But *Endgame* does not. *Endgame*
makes the music which *Eleuthéria* could only invoke.

Endgame is constructed in more or less clearly defined
sections which are 'played without a break'; the sections being
frequently marked off by pauses but never by an interval as
significant as that between the movements in a piece of
music. Hamm and Clov correspond constructionally less to
the 'characters' in a traditional play than to musical instru-
ments. Their special characteristics are not used in the development of a plot, but to carry as it were pitch and timbre,
to give off matching or dissonant tones and colours. If we
think of Hamm and Clov in the first instance as, for example,
'cello and violin instead of as two people that we might see
walking the streets; if we think of Nell and Nagg as, say, a pair
of flutes; we are already closer to understanding the construction of the play. This can be summarized as follows:
short solo prologues for Clov and Hamm (p. 12) lead into
an extended duo for both (pp. 13–18) which is joined briefly
by Nagg (pp. 15–16). Then comes a duo for Nagg and Nell,
with occasional interjections from Hamm and a solo passage
for Nagg (pp. 18–22). A second long duo for Hamm and
Clov (pp. 22–34), including two solo flourishes for Hamm
(p. 28 and p. 32), is broken by a short recitative for Hamm
and Nagg (p. 35) before Hamm embarks on his central
cadenza (pp. 35–7). A short trio for Hamm, Nagg and Clov
ends with Nagg's second and last solo passage (pp. 37–9).
At this point, with Hamm's stolen words 'Our revels now are

ended', the play seems to embark on its finale, a duo for Hamm and Clov, punctuated by a solo passage for each and finishing with an epilogue for Hamm.

Within these main sections of the play scraps of material are introduced which are sometimes stated simply in a single line, sometimes tossed from one character-instrument to another over several lines of dialogue between two pauses, but which almost always recur throughout the play. The second sentence of Clov's solo prologue is: 'Grain upon grain, one by one, and one day, suddenly, there's a heap, a little heap, the impossible heap' (p. 12). This material only recurs directly once more, when it is given to Hamm, in his solo passage during the finale: 'Moment upon moment, pattering down, like the millet grains of . . . (*he hesitates*) . . . that old Greek, and all life long you wait for that to mount up to a life' (p. 45). The identity of the old Greek – Beckett himself only remembers him to be one of the pre-Socratic philosophers, but not Zeno – is less germane than the fact that his image re-echoes across thirty-odd pages of the text and between Hamm and Clov, with perhaps half-heard reminders at other points in the play: during the first duo when Hamm asks Clov 'Did your seeds come up?' (p. 17) and in Hamm's cadenza (his 'story'), 'Corn, yes, I have corn, it's true, in my granaries' (p. 36).

The 'pain-killer' which Hamm asks for during his first duo with Clov (p. 14) recurs in the same duo (p. 16), three times in their second duo (pp. 23, 28, and 34) and again in the finale (p. 46). But the form of its final recurrence, in Clov's words 'There's no more pain-killer,' links it to several other diverse strands of material: 'There are no more bicycle-wheels' and 'There's no more pap' in the first duo (p. 15), 'There are no more sugar-plums' in the trio (p. 38), 'There's no more tide' (p. 41), 'There are no more rugs' (p. 44), 'There are no more coffins' (p. 49) in the finale.

In addition to this type of material – the subject-matter of conversation – there are the physical objects, the stage-properties, such as the telescope, the gaff, the toy dog with three legs, the step-ladder, which also recur from one section of the play to another. Then there are catch-phrases, such as Clov's constantly repeated 'I'll leave you' and 'I have things to do' or Hamm's 'Me to play' and 'We're getting on' which recall the little windings up or windings down with which composers cross from one musical plateau to another.

More remarkable still are the longer passages which seem to reflect one another across the play, but elusively, with certain distortions, as though refracted in water. In his central cadenza Hamm tells a story, complete with embellishments in a 'narrative tone', about a man who 'came crawling towards me, on his belly', his face 'black with mingled dirt and tears' and who asked for bread to take back to his little boy, 'as if the sex mattered'. Hamm tells how he offered to take the man into his service, since 'he had touched a chord', but leaves it doubtful whether he consented to take in the boy too (pp. 35–7). Earlier in the play Hamm has said to Clov: 'It was I was a father to you' and 'My house a home for you' (p. 29), while just before the end Clov sees through one of the windows, with the aid of the telescope, what he says 'Looks like a small boy!' Whether or not these three elements can be made to bear a rational concatenation is an open question. Their function in the play is to lack definition when placed one on top of the other, while remaining, each in itself, as clear as glass; and in this way they create an effect of mystery, a situation comparable to life itself in which, as Beckett said in an interview with Tom Driver, we are aware simultaneously of things that are obscure and things that are clear.

In one of Hamm's solo flourishes we are given what seems to be a reflection of the whole play, but seen in miniature from a long way off, as though at the wrong end of a telescope:

I once knew a madman who thought the end of the world had come. He was a painter – and engraver. I had a great fondness for him. I used to go and see him, in the asylum. I'd take him by the hand and drag him to the window. Look! There! All that rising corn! And there! Look! The sails of the herring-fleet! All that loveliness! (*Pause.*) He'd snatch away his hand and go back into his corner. Appalled. All he had seen was ashes. (*Pause.*) He alone had been spared. (*Pause.*) Forgotten. (*Pause.*) It appears the case is . . . was not so . . . so unusual.

(Endgame, p. 32)

In his final solo passage Clov seems to be seeing the same reflection, though with the eyes of the painter-engraver and so of course with all the pictorial elements burned away:

They said to me, Here's the place, stop, raise your head and look at all that beauty. That order! They said to me, Come now, you're not a brute beast, think upon these things and you'll see how all becomes clear. And simple! They said to me, What skilled attention they get, all these dying of their wounds . . . I open the door of the cell and go. I am so bowed I only see my feet, if I open my eyes, and between my legs a little trail of black dust. I say to myself that the earth is extinguished, though I never saw it lit. (*Endgame*, pp. 50–1)

This complex web of references, recurrences, reflections might easily turn into a mere tangle. It is given coherence by the play's dominant and almost absurdly simple theme, which is stated in the opening sentence of Clov's prologue: 'Finished, it's finished, nearly finished, it must be nearly finished.' Two sentences later Clov gives the theme his own thin timbre – 'I can't be punished any more' – and five sentences after that Hamm plays it with a kind of hollow, if mellow, grandeur: 'Can there be misery – (*he yawns*) – loftier than mine?' Nagg's laconic opening squeak is 'Me pap!' and Nell, perhaps more of an oboe than a flute, having failed to kiss Nagg, says: 'Why this farce, day after day?' Then, discarding almost immediately this bold, practical tone in favour

of another, which Beckett characterizes as 'elegiac', she re-
states the theme: 'Ah yesterday!' Thereafter she alternates
between the practical and the elegiac.

The whole play is in effect a mass of variations on the
theme, variations of material, variations between solo, duo
and ensemble, variations of tone between one character
and another and within a single character, variations of pace
and mood (comic, tragic, bombastic, maudlin, etc.). There
could hardly be an easier play to grasp the drift of – the
title alone tells all. If it is, as Beckett says it is, 'more difficult
. . . more inhuman than *Godot*', the difficulty is emotional,
aesthetic. *Endgame* can only be enjoyed, understood in the
emotional sense, through its presentation, which is as complex, as many-layered and multiple, as its theme is simple and
single. And when Beckett uses the word 'inhuman', which
might tend to confirm the worst prejudices of those for whom
the word 'human' has become as much a moral cliché as
'gentleman' once was, we should perhaps take it in the rather
Wildean sense suggested by M Krap in *Eleuthéria*:

MME PIOUK. You used to be natural.
M KRAP. By dint of what artifice!   (*Eleuthéria*, p. 27)

The four character-instruments of *Endgame* have given
much food for thought to Beckett's commentators. Hamm is
Hamlet and a ham-actor and the son of Noah, also the ham
that comes from a pig and Clov his clove; Hamm is the
hammer, Clov the French nail (*clou*), Nagg the German nail
(*Nagel*), Nell the English nail. Bearing in mind Beckett's
remark in *Proust* that 'name is an example of a barbarous
society's primitivism, and as conventionally inadequate as
"Homer" or "sea" ', we would probably do best to look
upon the characters' names as deliberately blurred labels, more
succinctly blurred than, for example, Vladimir in *Waiting for
Godot*, who is called 'Didi' by his companion and 'Mr Albert'
by Godot's messenger-boy. As to who the characters may be

and what their relationship with each other, no commentator has better expressed the matter than H.R.H. The Duke of Windsor:

> Sometimes when my father admonished me for something that I had done with 'My dear boy, you must always remember who you are,' I used to think: Now, who am I? No answer.
> (Interview with Kenneth Harris)

Just as the construction of *Endgame* can be most easily understood by analogy with music, so the characters lend themselves to an analogy with painting. Their special characteristics as well as the relationships between them are like layers of different-coloured pigment superimposed on one another, set off against one another, to produce a rich texture and a balanced composition. Unlike the sections into which the play as a whole is divided, and the sections within sections, all of which are clearly marked off by pauses, the superimposed elements which make up the characters constantly blend into one another, so that it is quite often difficult to tell which characteristic is uppermost, which relationship operating.

Clov's most prominent characteristics are clearly painted in from the start: his opening mime and the prologue that follows it show him to be in a subservient, or at least attendant, position, and to be a person without illusions. His appearance, his manner of walking and the 'business' of his mime (fetching, carrying, ascending, descending, re-ascending, re-descending a step-ladder, forgetting it and returning for it) suggest the Clown, while his 'brief laugh', his toneless and almost savage prologue say Feste or Lear's Fool rather than Bottom or Touchstone. Yet it is Clov, 'motionless by the door, his eyes fixed on Hamm', who opens and closes the play, it is he who draws back the curtains from the two windows and removes the dust-sheets covering Hamm in his chair and Nell and Nagg in the dustbins; the kitchen table on

which he tells us he leans off stage looking at the wall, hints
at being an author's table. 'And what do you see on your wall?'
Hamm asks him a little further on, 'Mene, Mene? Naked
bodies?' to which Clov replies with studied lack of definition: 'I see my light dying.' Certainly he attends upon Hamm
and comes to his whistle, but so does an author attend upon
his characters when they summon him from the dreary
contemplation of his blank wall; certainly he wishes he might
kill his character and finish the comedy, but that is a desire
we have observed in all Beckett's authorial characters. Clov,
at any rate, is a more easily put-upon, more helpless author
than Pirandello's in *Six Characters in Search of an Author*.
Why are they in search of an author in the first place? Because, in the Father's words, their original author 'sought to
deny them life', left them 'unrealised', even when, as the
Stepdaughter says:

> I would go and tempt him . . . There, in his gloomy study
> . . . Just at twilight . . . He would be sitting there, sunk in an
> armchair . . . Not bothering to stir himself and switch on the
> light . . . Content to let the room get darker and darker . . .
> Until the whole room was filled with a darkness that was alive
> with our presence . . . We were there to tempt him . . .
>
> (*Six Characters in Search of an Author*, tr. Frederick May)

But then in the 'grey light' of *Endgame* Clov's character
Hamm is a tougher proposition altogether than the Six
Characters. Unlike the Father and Stepdaughter, who when
they come to act out their scene do so in inaudible whispers
and who are appalled when they see actors playing their
roles, Hamm is as much actor as character. 'Me to play' he
begins at once and apostrophizes the blood-stained handkerchief he has just removed from his face as 'Old stancher!',
then taking the bit between his teeth: 'Can there be misery
loftier than mine?' Hamm is not the sort of character an author
can put out on the streets, not with his blind eyes (or at least
dark glasses) and that heavily conscious reference to most of

the heroes of Tragedy: 'Woe, woe is me! Miserable, miserable
that I am!' (*Oedipus Rex*); 'Ah, this is one misery I have not
yet endured. What fresh torments still lie in wait for me?'
(Racine's *Phèdre*); 'As full of grief as age; wretched in both'
(*King Lear*); 'Appease the misery of the living and the re-
morse of the dead' (Yeats's *Purgatory*); 'We carry within
ourselves a terrible and grievous drama' (*Six Characters*).
He is not even content to hog the tragic role, but insists on
providing his own comic relief: 'Can there be misery loftier
than mine? No doubt. Formerly.' He is an adept at this
kind of combined attack and defence, the hammer blow of
tragedy at the same time as the defensives stroke of parody:
'My kingdom for a nightman!' and 'Our revels now are
ended. The dog's gone.' He will be not only Richard III,
Prospero, Oedipus, but also an Oedipus perfectly aware that
his audience is a *bourgeois* one and can better stomach comedy
than tragedy. Anxious as he is to arouse pity and terror in
his hearers, he is not willing to forfeit thereby their sensible
respect for him as a man-of-the-world. Hence the deflationary
asides, the yawns and cynicisms with which he peppers his
flights of purple rhetoric.

Nagg, on the other hand, his 'accursed progenitor', makes
no pretence at tragic dignity. He, it is clear from his anecdote
of the tailor and the pair of trousers (pp. 21–2) with its carefully paid-out string of mild obscenities, has never aimed at
any performance grander than the after-dinner speech at
some low-powered convention. The tables are turned on
him, he receives his own particular purgatorial bridle, when
he is bribed (he never collects the bribe) to listen to Hamm's
story, though as he says afterwards – equating Hamm's story
with Mr Endon's game of chess – 'you didn't really need to
have me listen to you. Besides I didn't listen to you.' It is to
Nell perhaps that Hamm owes his romanticism, though hers
is pale and reedy by comparison with Hamm's sunset *vox
humana*.

In addition to playing Hamm's long-suffering author, Clov has the further misfortune to be on stage with him in the role of straight man and confidant – a situation which he supports only with incessant complaint and a whole repertoire of naked contempt for his principal. And just as this relationship of actor to actor is superimposed on the basic one of author to character, so other relationships are superimposed in their turn: servant and master, son and father, nurse and invalid. Sometimes Hamm and Clov seem to be the survivors of some global disaster. They often speak as if all life beyond their 'refuge' had ended, they are alarmed at the appearance of a rat in Clov's kitchen and a flea in Clov's trousers (though this rat and flea also bring us back to Clov's authorship and Hamm's actorship, with their reference, taken together, to the drinking scene in Goethe's *Faust*). The little boy whom Clov sees through the window near the end of the play is perhaps another, unexpected, survivor, though he may also be ('potential procreator', as Clov calls him) an enemy pawn crawling towards the back line to become a Queen, since Hamm and Clov are apt to look like chesspieces in some lights and the whole affair quite literally an endgame on a chequered board. Then again it could be the love-affair of Hamm and his handkerchief ('old stancher') or of Clov and the contents of his own head, with Hamm representing Clov himself in more imaginative guise and the two windows Clov's eyes which see the 'big world' outside only as a double desolation of earth and water.

To attempt to force the whole play into any one of these 'meanings' would be as meaningless as to try to force a painting into the meaning of one of its many layers of paint. Nevertheless there is one enigma which requires an answer, since it concerns the effect of the play on its audience. Why, when every prospect within the play has been so devastatingly bleak, when, whatever else we cannot say about it, we can undoubtedly say we have witnessed an endgame, something attempting to coil itself to a close and just failing (as Mr Endon's King just failed to step back into his own square), why do we feel so exhilarated as we leave the theatre? In his study of Proust, Beckett discusses Habit and writes:

> The pendulum oscillates between these two terms: Suffering – that opens a window on the real and is the main condition of the artistic experience, and Boredom – with its host of top-hatted and hygienic ministers, Boredom that must be considered as the most tolerable because the most durable of human evils.
>
> (*Proust*, p. 28)

And he goes on:

> I draw the conclusion of this matter from Proust's treasury of nutshell phrases: 'If there were no such thing as Habit, Life would of necessity appear delicious to all those whom Death would threaten at every moment, that is to say, to all Mankind'.
>
> (*Proust*, p. 29)

In *Endgame*, we have participated with Clov in his suffering and Hamm in his boredom, with Clov in his boredom and Hamm very occasionally in his suffering ('no more pain-killer'), but we have also, after the curious fashion of a theatrical experience, been all the time in our seats and received with our own senses the unique shape that Beckett has made. Within the play we have experienced Habit, but in a manner the very reverse of habitual. So unhabitual has it been that we have actually confronted the banal certainty of death as though for the first time. No wonder that, if only for a moment, life appears delicious.

5

Love and Doom in an Irish Suburb

ALL THAT FALL (1957)

Beckett's first excursion into radio drama is not only notable in its confident annexation of a fresh medium, it is also striking for an unusual (for him) degree of definition in its setting. In fact it is – curiously – a rather naturalistic play, written for a medium almost by definition non-naturalistic. In radio work there are no spatial dimensions (*All That Fall* was in any case written before the spread of stereophony), only the temporal one. Voices must be clearly differentiated in timbre if they are not to be confused, so that Beckett's relatively large cast of eleven speakers is a gesture of defiance, a characteristic refusal to accept limitations timidly. Sound-effects are always a problem (real boots treading genuine gravel may not come across authentically like an electronic artefact simulating the gravelly crunch), and Beckett requires several natural – which means unnatural – noises, notably of sheep, bird, cow, cock, dragging feet, wind and rain. But the medium offers him distinct compensatory advantages: the silences are complete silences, total suspensions of activity such as are impossible of achievement on the stage, and the worn and dusty record of 'Death and the Maiden', which serves as a link between the two ends of the play, comes over poignantly concrete, being both free of the irrelevant distractions of visible reproduction machinery and more immediate than a ghostly sound off stage. 'Silence but for music playing' (p. 7), an early direction, is typical indeed of the serial thinking radio drama imposes, of its curious kind of sonorous cause and effect, as is the following instance also: 'Give her a good welt on the rump. (*Sound of welt. Pause.*) Harder! (*Sound of welt. Pause.*) Well! If someone were to do that for me I should not dally' (p. 8). The extraordinary precision of conception within a symbolic framework which is so characteristic of Beckett's vision is thus particularly well equipped to take full advantage of the strengths as well as the limitations of radio drama. So that 'jangle of bicycle bell' constitutes the arrival of Mr Tyler on his bicycle, and 'squeak of brakes' his slowing down abreast of Maddy: aural commotion *is* action, since reality demands no other basis than sound. And Beckett can in consequence exploit radio's potential for ironic commentary: when Mrs Rooney asks in one of her tearful moments, 'What did I do with that handkerchief?' she is deflated shrewdly, if affectionately, by the direction immediately following: 'Sound of handkerchief loudly applied' (p. 17). This, like the pseudo-farmyard noises, makes up one of the dimensions of Beckett's wit, to which I shall return later.

For the moment let us pursue the technical aspect, bearing in mind that radio drama creates a purely aural world. The setting of *All That Fall* is an Irish suburb, Boghill, around noon on a Saturday of changeable summer weather. The social milieu is that of Protestant middle-class commuters, and the only local event of consequence occupying their thoughts is the race meeting to be held that afternoon – 'divine day for the meeting' is a characteristic form of greeting. This is, in fact, the world in which Beckett grew up, and knows intimately, whence the slightly old-fashioned air that makes the play something of an exercise in nostalgia: a penny is an appropriate tip to a helpful boy, for example, and seven and six a day enough to keep a man 'alive and twitching' (p. 30). The play proper consists of a series of episodes. Fat Maddy Rooney is on her way to Boghill station to meet her blind husband Dan off the train which brings him from his city office. She is overtaken first by Christy the carter, who asks her if she's in need of a small load of dung. Then Mr Tyler, a retired bill-broker, comes by on his way to meet Hardy the curate off the same train, and Connolly's van nearly runs them over as it roars past. Next her old flame Mr Slocum, clerk of the race-course, pulls up and offers her a lift. On her arrival at the station she is helped out of Slocum's car by Tommy the porter, engages in conversation with Mr Barrell the station-master and is given an arm up the platform steps by Miss Fitt. After considerable delay, the city train pulls in, and Dan and Maddy make their way home together in worsening weather, passing the 'lovely laburnum' which Maddy had admired on her way in, and briefly discuss the dung question raised by Christy. The symmetry of dramatic conception, so characteristic of Beckett, might lead us to expect a close as uneventful as the opening, were it not for the unexpected arrival of Jerry, the small boy who guides Mr Rooney to and from the station every day, but who on this occasion was not needed (to Dan's annoyance) since Maddy had come herself as a surprise on her husband's birthday. Jerry has run after them to return something Mr Rooney had dropped – a kind of ball – and despite the old man's protests tells Maddy the reason the twelve-thirty was late: 'It was a little child fell out of the carriage, Ma'am. On the line, Ma'am. Under the wheels, Ma'am.' The play ends at that point, the enigma of the child's death unresolved.

But as we think back over what we have heard, we recall certain clues. The Rooneys had lost their only daughter, Minnie, many years before, and the memory of their bereavement makes them both unhappy. 'In her forties now she'd be,' Maddy recalls brokenly, 'girding up her lovely little loins, getting ready for the change' (p. 12), and Dan weeps as he recognizes the sombre melody from Schubert's 'Death and the Maiden' quartet. Earlier, in his anger at the Lynch twins jeering at them, he asks Maddy, 'Did you ever wish to kill a child? Nip some young doom in the bud' (p. 28), and confides that 'many a time at night, in winter, on the black road home, I nearly attacked the boy'. Later, they join together in bitter laughter over the text from Psalm 145 which gives the play its title and which is to be preached next day: 'The Lord up-holdeth all that fall and raiseth up all those that be bowed down' (p. 36). To take revenge on God for fallacious promises and for taking Minnie from them, it is implied, Mr Rooney perhaps pushed another person's child to a premature death on the line he felt himself this fateful birthday to be travelling once too often. Salvation, in fact, is a deceit, not a going 'home' to a 'higher life' as the devout Miss Fitt believes. All that man can expect is 'silly unhappiness' (p. 17), and the meagre consolation of arithmetic, here called 'one of the few satisfactions in life' (p. 27) perhaps because, as Beckett's master Descartes found three centuries before, properly con-ducted calculations can lead even an infant to such rare cer-tainties as are sparsely accessible to human reason. Apart from this rather limited form of satisfaction, the outlook is bleak. Love is doomed to sterility, and death lies in wait for everyone, and not only those who, like the little girl Mrs Rooney once heard a psychiatrist lecture on, have 'never been really born' (p. 34).

Sterility, in fact, is something of an obsession with these Irish suburbanites. Mr Tyler's daughter has had 'the whole . . . er . . . bag of tricks' removed, leaving him 'grandchild-less', which perhaps is no bad thing since Tyler himself has survived only to 'curse God and man and the wet Saturday afternoon of my conception' (p. 10). Now another wet Satur-day afternoon is upon them with its abhorred potential for occasioning other misconceptions, subsequently liable to be similarly cursed by their unfortunate benefactors. When

Mr Slocum squashes a hen, Mrs Rooney is consoled at the
thought that at least for one of God's creatures 'all the laying
and the hatching' are at an end (p. 15). For those that remain,
the sole prospect held out is of 'a lingering dissolution . . .
wasting slowly, painlessly away' (pp. 10, 16). Maddy, in particular, is conscious of this. She congratulates Miss Fitt on her
truly piercing sight, since it makes of Mrs Rooney *née* Dunne
merely 'a big pale blur' or, at best, 'a once female shape'
(pp. 18–19).

   This all-pervasive note of sterility infects love itself, something in which Maddy struggles still to believe: 'Love, that is
all I asked, a little love, daily, twice daily, fifty years of twice
daily love like a Paris horse-butcher's regular, what normal
woman wants affection?' she asks. She rejects wobbly Mr
Tyler's request to lay his hand lightly on her shoulder, being
tired of 'light old hands on my shoulders and other senseless
places' (pp. 9–10). When he has been driven off by her sharp-
ness, she regrets his (albeit mild) masculine presence: the
cooing of 'Venus birds' in the woods prompts her to hyster-
ical bawdy laughter as she tries to recall him to unlace her
behind the hedge. She titters girlishly as Mr Slocum (obscene
pun intended) puts his shoulder to her rear to hoist her into
his car. Dan reproves her sternly when she giggles that 'it will
be like old times' if they fall together into the ditch on their
way home (p. 26), but he is not immune himself to erotic
fantasy. 'You will read to me,' he gloats, 'I think Effie is
going to commit adultery with the Major' (p. 26); but the
reference to Fontane's great tragic novel *Effi Briest* (1895) is
ironic, since its treatment of a young wife's transgression is so
discreetly oblique that most readers miss it altogether on first
reading. But even Krapp believed he could have made Effi a
better lover than her cavalry officer did 'up there on the Baltic,
and the pines, and the dunes' (*Krapp's Last Tape*, p. 17). There
is spark enough of amorousness left in Dan, however, for him
to earn Maddy's gratitude by putting his arm round her

and being 'nice' to her in one of the play's gentler moments
(p. 35).

Otherwise he is, he maintains, only half-alive. In his loving
contemplation of decay he reminds us of Malone, except that
he is blessed with a drier wit:

> Well! Did you ever know me to be well? The day you met me
> I should have been in bed. The day you proposed to me the
> doctors gave me up. You knew that, did you not? The night you
> married me they came for me with an ambulance. You have not
> forgotten that, I suppose? No, I cannot be said to be well. But
> I am no worse. Indeed I am better than I was. The loss of my
> sight was a great fillip.   (*All That Fall*, p. 29)

The leitmotif, in fact, is the notion of bentness ironically referred to in the preacher's text and picked up elsewhere. 'You
are bent all double', Maddy is told by Mr Slocum (p. 12), and
she informs blind Dan that he is 'bowed down over the ditch'
(p. 34). Beckett's extraordinary sensitivity to language, here
made to pattern a theme, is perhaps attributable in part to the
fact that this was the first play written in his mother Anglo-
Irish, which his characters wrestle with uncomfortably. 'Do
you know, Maddy,' Dan says, 'sometimes one would think
you were struggling with a dead language' (pp. 31–2), and
she herself finds something 'bizarre' about her way of speaking. The complexities of English syntax give even the confident Dan cause to hesitate: 'for which is there?' somehow
'does not sound right' to him as a response to 'there is nothing
to be done for those people' (p. 34). But before English goes
the way of 'our own poor dear Gaelic' it can be handled with
amazing virtuosity and wit. Of Hardy Mr Tyler says 'I saved
his life once', not omitting to add 'I have not forgotten it', and
Mrs Rooney twists Grey of Fallodon when she quips, 'this
dust will not settle in our time' (p. 11). The 'distray' Miss
Fitt (pun again intended) eats her doily instead of the thin
bread and butter, and fails to catch Mr Tyler's innuendo about
the 'bawdy hour of nine – or three alas' (p. 22).

Radio is an ideal medium for verbal humour of this kind, since the listener's attention is undivided, as the success of British comedy series from *Itma* to the *Goon Show* has abundantly proved. Beckett was not slow to exploit these possibilities to the full, and create in *All That Fall* one of his wittiest pieces. It is this comedy, shot through with sadness at decline and fall, which helps explain why the play is one of his most satisfying dramatic statements. And the violent mystery of Jerry's closing words presents the hearer with a problem not easily resolved – one perhaps more painful to sustain than the blank stare of two men waiting at a roadside for a saviour unable to keep his appointment; one certainly more powerfully concrete as the medium of wireless is baselessly immaterial, an insubstantial pageant which leaves its enigmas entire.

6

Death and the Maiden

KRAPP'S LAST TAPE (1958)

Sheltered under his most rebarbative title – with its triple allusion to excrement, dissolution and machinery – lies Beckett's most lyrical and tender play. John Fletcher has recorded, in an article in *Modern Drama*, that Roger Blin, the original director of *Waiting for Godot*:

> . . . had several things to say about the author of the play. The cruelty in his work was, he maintained, a form of self-defence against an acute sensibility, and he told how, once going through the quarter of Les Halles in Paris with Beckett, he noticed how the latter started on seeing animal heads and offal in a cart, and how much the sight of blood affected him.

It was, of course, Krapp's almost namesake, M Henri Krap in *Eleuthéria*, who called himself 'the cow which at the gates of the slaughterhouse, realises all the absurdity of pastures'. Beckett takes care not to soften his new Krapp's shell: the play opens with the almost stock Beckettian clown's routine – on this occasion it is a bit of business with a banana – while the character's most noticeable external characteristics are an addiction to alcohol, a violent temper and a withered lechery.

Nevertheless, *Krapp's Last Tape* shares with its neighbouring works (the short prose-piece *From an Abandoned Work*, begun in 1955, and the radio play *Embers*, written in 1959) a mood of nostalgia, an atmosphere of the pastoral and idyllic, an unashamedly poetic idiom. The three works seem to develop around *All That Fall* (1956) and to form a kind of triptych on the theme of lost love in an Irish landscape. But whereas in *All That Fall* this landscape was deliberately formal, almost dinky, in the manner of a naïve painting – every sound-effect constantly asserted the fact that it was a sound-effect – it has become in *Krapp's Last Tape* and the other two works of the 'triptych' something internal to the characters, evocative, romantic, personal. And whereas the characters in *All That Fall* were moving through their landscape as it were in public, seen (or rather heard) from outside, so that their preoccupation with the very same theme, the loss of love, appeared in a somewhat guarded, conversational form – natural to those in the presence of other people – the characters in the triptych are alone and can let themselves go. Their characteristics, that is to say, resemble in many ways those of Mr and Mrs Rooney, just as their landscape does, but their situation is that of the absent character in *All That Fall*, the 'Poor woman. All alone in that ruinous house', whose single endlessly repeated record of Schubert's 'Death and the Maiden' quartet impinges faintly and momentarily on the Rooneys' outward and return journeys.

'Death and the Maiden' is the burden of Krapp's tape: his

own recorded voice at the age of thirty-nine recounts, among other things, the death of his mother and an incident with a girl in a punt. Krapp himself, the sole human occupant of the stage, is now sixty-nine and sits 'front centre' at the table bearing his tape recorder and its spools 'in strong white light', the rest of the stage being dark. Things were like this even thirty years ago when he recorded the tape, for his thirty-nine-year-old voice remarks: 'The new light above my table is a great improvement. With all this darkness round me I feel less alone.' But according to Martin Held, who plays the part of Krapp in the famous Berlin Schiller Theater production (which was directed by Beckett), this darkness contains the promise of something more than mere companionship for the living sixty-nine-year-old Krapp. In an interview in *The Times* Held spoke about working with Beckett:

> He often went into detail. For instance when Krapp looks backward – you remember? When he's about to switch the machine on and he thinks he hears something behind him and he listens and slowly turns round. I knew just what Beckett meant when he said 'Old Nick's there. Death is standing behind him and unconsciously he's looking for it.'

In the poem by Matthias Claudius which Schubert first set as a song, later using the music as the theme of his slow movement in the D minor Quartet (the movement the old woman in *All That Fall* is listening to), Death's words are: 'Be of good courage, I am not wild, you will slumber gently in my arms.' Thus, like the old woman in the ruinous house, Krapp sits in his 'den' listening to his personal version of 'Death and the Maiden' and waiting for Death to claim him, though not, as Beckett impressed on Held, with any feeling of resignation. Krapp is not maiden in the strictest sense – his thirty-year-old tape refers to 'living on and off with Bianca in Kedar Street' and when he comes to recording his latest tape he confides to the microphone: 'Fanny came in a couple of times. Bony old ghost of a whore' – but he has been incapable of love, of receiving it or of giving it. It is in this sense that all Beckett's heroes suffer the loss of love, not from misfortune, like Romeo and Juliet, not from the interference of others, like Heloise and Abelard, but from personal incapacity. Krapp says of Bianca: 'Well out of that, Jesus yes! Hopeless business,' and even of the girl in the punt, the very centre of his idyll: 'I said again I thought it was hopeless and no good going on and she agreed, without opening her eyes.'

The brilliant theatrical device on which the play is constructed, which enables present to confront past and past to confront present, is not of course unprecedented in the theatre. Yeats, for instance, used it in his play about Swift, *Words on the Windowpane*, and to much greater effect in *Purgatory*, whose two characters, an old man and his son, and their unhappy relationship must certainly have influenced many of Beckett's characters, including Hamm and Clov. But Beckett's particular use of the device in *Krapp's Last Tape*, so that Krapp is actually present in both his selves at the same time and in the same place, his thirty-nine-year-old self encapsulated on the tape and his sixty-nine-year-old self listening to it, gives signs of being borrowed directly from another of Schubert's famous settings, Heine's poem *Der Doppelgänger*:

> The night is still, the streets are quiet,
> In this house lived the girl I loved;
> She left the city long ago,
> But the house is standing where it stood.
> And a man is standing, staring up,
> Twisting his hands, in agony;
> I'm shivering now – I see his face –
> The moonlit features are my own.
> You my double! You pale thing!
> Why do you ape my love, my pain,
> The hurts I suffered in this place
> So many nights, so long ago?

Krapp's *doppelgänger* on the tape tells how he sat on a bench
by the canal keeping watch on the house and the window
inside which 'mother lay a-dying, in the late autumn, after her
long viduity' and 'wishing she were gone'. He tells how he
attempted to accost a nursemaid 'all white and starch, in-
comparable bosom' and was repulsed, how at the moment
when his mother's blind went down he was throwing a small
black ball for a dog and how the dog took the ball in its
mouth: 'I shall feel it, in my hand, until my dying day!' To all
this the living Krapp listens with attention, switching the tape
off once to look up 'viduity' in a dictionary and again to brood
over the nursemaid's face, but visibly unmoved. He has been
equally unmoved, except to the occasional 'brief laugh', by
his *doppelgänger*'s earlier reminiscences, but it is a measure of
how much this play needs to be experienced in the theatre,
rather than simply read, that these double laughs – the laughs
of middle-aged Krapp on the tape, accompanied by the laughs
of old Krapp on the stage, culminating in a laugh from the old
Krapp which is not shared by him of the tape – have a literally
hair-raising effect on an audience. Brecht said of his own
theatre: 'I am laughing about those who weep on the stage,
weeping about those who laugh.' The extra dimension, then,
that Beckett has added to Heine's poem, and it is what makes
Krapp's Last Tape a play rather than a dramatic poem, is to
put the two selves out of focus with each other – both are in
agony, the causes of the agony are the same, but it is not the
same agony.

One of the differences between them becomes apparent in
the passage on the tape which follows that of the mother's
death. Krapp-on-the-tape speaks of 'that memorable night in
March, at the end of the jetty, in the howling wind, never to
be forgotten, when suddenly I saw the whole thing. The
vision at last' (p. 15). A few moments later he starts to explain
what he means: 'What I suddenly saw then was this, that the
belief I had been going on all my life, namely –' and again a

few moments later: 'clear to me at last that the dark I have always struggled to keep under is in reality my most –' These fractured lucidities alternate with over-excited, flushed romantic images taken at breakneck speed: 'for the fire that set it alight . . . great granite rocks the foam flying up in the light of the lighthouse and the wind-gauge spinning like a propeller . . . unshatterable association until my dissolution of storm and night with the light of the understanding and the fire'.

But we never receive a full explanation of Krapp-on-the-tape's 'vision', since the passage rouses the old, living Krapp to a frenzy of cursing and winding the tape forward. Krapp is, has been a writer. When the old Krapp stops listening and comes to make his own latest tape, he tells his microphone: 'Seventeen copies sold, of which eleven at trade price to free circulating libraries beyond the seas. Getting known.' Only one writer's pleasure remains to old Krapp: 'Revelled in the word spool.' Whether or not the thirty-nine-year-old Krapp's vision corresponds to a vision of Beckett's own – the two certainly seem to bear certain resemblances, both in point of age and so far as can be judged in point of content, as I have suggested in the introduction (p. 28) – its juxtaposition with the sixty-nine-year-old Krapp's sales makes it sufficiently agonizing from both points of view.

The matter, however, does not rest there. The passage at which old Krapp arrives when he has finished winding on his middle-aged effusions is the one describing the incident of the girl in the punt. The mood is delicately lyrical, the scene is bathed in sunlight, the lines evoke as they describe: 'We drifted in among the flags and stuck. The way they went down, sighing, before the stem!' (p. 16). There is an atmosphere of sexual ardour, which stops short of the crudely animal but which is if anything heightened by the poet-lover's tinge of melancholy: 'I said again I thought it was hopeless and no good going on and she agreed.' Everything is as different as possible from old Krapp's summary a few minutes later of his

recent encounter with Fanny, the bony old ghost of a whore:
'Couldn't do much, but I suppose better than a kick in the
crutch.' Yet old Krapp does not wind the tape forward when
he hears middle-aged Krapp's lyric; on the contrary, he winds
it back to hear more of the beginning and then, having
abandoned his own fresh recording on a note of bitter nostalgia, suddenly puts middle-aged Krapp's tape back on the
machine and plays the whole 'punt' passage through once more.

But this time he omits to switch off after the passage, so that
the play ends with our hearing for the first time the epilogue
to middle-aged Krapp's tape: 'Perhaps my best years are gone.
When there was a chance of happiness. But I wouldn't want
them back. Not with the fire in me now. No, I wouldn't want
them back' (p. 19). The agony of old Krapp is that he does
want them back and never mind the 'fire' which sold him
seventeen copies. The sentiment is again Heine's who, like
Malone in Beckett's novel *Malone Dies*, lay writing on his
'mattress-grave' in Paris:

> Dead and cold in my heart
> Is every empty earthly want,
> Even my hatred for the bad, the rotten,
> Is dead and cold, and my sense of misery,
> My own and other people's misery –
> The only thing alive in me now is death.

> The curtain falls, the play is over,
> And my kind German public
> Is tacking home, yawning;
> Those good people aren't stupid:
> They'll be putting back a decent meal now,
> Drinking their glassful, singing and laughing –
> He was right, the golden Hero,
> The one who said in Homer's book:
> The least little philistine nobody alive
> In Stukkert-am-Neckar is happier
> Than I am, Achilles, the dead general,
> Prince of shadows in the kingdom of hell.

7

Hectoring Voices in the Head

We remarked that *All That Fall* sought to create a three-dimensional world through techniques of aural illusion, and so in despite of its origin revealed analogies with stage drama. *Embers*, Beckett's second radio play, is more consistent in its exploitation of the medium: the world of its protagonist Henry is firmly interiorized, since the sounds he hears (and we hear) are mainly in his head. The same is true of Joe, in the more recent television play which explores a similar issue, except that the visual dimension inevitably removes the element of ambiguity as to the precise provenance of sounds that helps to explain why *Embers* is such an intriguing work (in Roger Blin's opinion, Beckett's finest).

As *Embers* opens, we hear sea and Henry's boots on the shingle. But we soon discover that the sea booms in Henry's head continually. He tries to drown it by talking aloud to himself and even by taking a gramophone with him wherever he goes; or else he summons up the beat of hooves, a dripping tap, clashes stones together, or just dreams of living in the Pampas far from its roar. 'I once went to Switzerland to get away from the cursed thing' he recalls disgustedly at one point; his wife Ada asks 'what's wrong with it, it's a lovely peaceful gentle soothing sound, why do you hate it?', but the only solution she can suggest is 'there's something wrong with your brain, you ought to see Holloway' (pp. 21, 30). She 'visits' Henry in the sense that her voice is heard, but unlike her husband she makes no other audible sounds, slipping a shawl under him and sitting down beside him on the pebbles in total silence. It is soon apparent to the listener that she, like their daughter Addie heard suffering at the hands of music teacher and riding master, are figments of Henry's fertile aural imagination. This acute inner ear of his seems equipped with sophisticated studio devices for amplifying sounds to paroxysm before suddenly cutting them off; it can even evoke a memory by associated words. Ada's 'don't' in 'don't wet your good boots' recalls another 'don't' of twenty years before, a cry of reluctant acquiescence uttered in the hollow 'where we did it at last for the first time' (pp. 29, 31). Henry – this much is evident – alone makes the sounds that fill his dramatic universe. The way is clear for the creation of an 'opener' controlling the channels in a wholly imaginary studio of the mind; a natural step which Beckett takes in *Cascando*.

To drown the noise of the sea in his head, Henry has the resource of all Beckettian heroes. Malone, we recall, invented stories to prevent himself listening to the sounds of his dying, and Henry talks aloud to cover the seashell echo in his brain. The story he constructs is 'a great one about an old fellow called Bolton', and the episode he has reached concerns a visit paid by Dr Holloway at Bolton's request late one bitter winter's night as the embers are dying in the hearth (hence the play's title, although the fast-days of the Christian calendar are an associated reference). Like Hamm in *Endgame*, or Voice in *Cascando*, Henry never finishes this story, nor (he tells us) has he ever finished any other. But, again like Hamm, he cannot manage indefinitely without an audience for his narration, and so conjures up someone who knew him 'in the old days', in this case Ada. Before Ada, he had summoned his father, from whom he had never managed to extract a word. Ada is more co-operative, but her resources are not unlimited, and she leaves him after describing her only meeting with his father, whom she had last seen sitting on a rock looking out to sea. Henry continues Ada's narrative alone, but soon exhausts its possibilities and returns to Bolton and Holloway in the closing minutes of the play.

Bolton is one of the enigmas the listener is presented with. Did he call in Holloway to present him with a request for euthanasia? If so, then the parallel between Bolton and Henry's dead father is reinforced, in at least one respect. The father, it is hinted, took his own life:

> . . . That evening bathe you took once too often . . . We never found your body, you know, that held up probate an unconscionable time, they said there was nothing to prove you hadn't run away from us all and alive and well under a false name in the Argentine for example, that grieved mother greatly.
>
> (*Embers*, p. 21)

Perhaps Henry has become so weary of addressing his father and getting no response that he creates a father-figure in Bolton, who yields him little satisfaction either however. He certainly experiences a feeling of guilt in connection with his immediate ancestor, whose last words to him were 'a washout, that's all you are, a washout!' (at which, appropriately, Henry slams a door in his head). The memory is not a pleasant one; it provokes Henry to wish his mother really had washed him out, as he wishes his conjugal efforts with Ada had not been crowned with success 'in the end'. The emphasis on willed and accidental sterility is all-pervasive, a denial of the family bond that brings only unhappiness: Holloway's 'panhysterectomy at nine' is simply a more learned restatement of the excision of the 'whole bag of tricks' undergone by Tyler's daughter in *All That Fall*.

Henry's motto is 'every syllable is a second gained'. It applies equally well to Joe, another sufferer from the accusing voice heard in the head. *Eh Joe* is otherwise not really comparable with *Embers*: it's a much slighter play, bordering even on triviality. Joe is first seen by the television camera from behind, as he goes round his room drawing curtains and hangings, sealing off all the exits. The camera then turns to scrutinize his face with its unblinking eyes animated only by the tension of listening to the disembodied voice of a woman. It is a rather colourless voice, growing fainter as the play proceeds. The camera moves, nine times in all, but only when the voice pauses, and serves as the inquisitorial extension of the nagging words over the loudspeaker. Joe, gradually 'throttling the dead in his head', started with his father (shades of Henry) and went on to his mother, both long since gone. Ada's warning to Henry extends therefore to Joe:

> The time will come when no one will speak to you at all, not even complete strangers. You will be quite alone with your voice, there will be no other voice in the world but yours.
>
> (*Embers*, p. 33)

For Joe, paradoxically, needs his voices even as he destroys them. He is a decaying Don Juan who can still manage a 'slut' like Krapp's Fanny, but his career as a 'lifelong adorer' is at an end. The play consists of a painful reminder by an ex-mistress (who afterwards 'did all right') of his callous treatment of another girl: 'You know the one I mean, Joe . . . The green one . . . The narrow one . . . Always pale . . .' He is not allowed to forget how he bundled her into 'her Avoca sack . . . Her fingers fumbling with the big horn buttons . . . Ticket in your pocket for the first morning flight . . .' (p. 19), nor how she tried first to drown herself, then to cut her wrists, and finally, swallowing a tube of tablets out of unrequited love for him, how she buried her face in the pebbles, like Woburn in *Cascando*. There is a certain macabre humour about all this, but the impression that remains is of a sad evocation of the ungallantries of a 'dry rotten' heart and a 'penny farthing hell you call your mind' (pp. 16–17).

This work invites comparison with *Play*, but what it lacks

is *Play*'s complex ironies. This is not to say that it isn't a competent piece of television writing (it is, by any fair standard of what constitutes the norm of dramatic composition for the medium), but simply that it is little more. Judged by Beckett's own standards it's a slender playlet, making one point well enough but going no further. The decision to select, as the prosecution in the case of another and less fortunate woman, one of Joe's happily resettled cast-off's, leads Beckett into a rare lapse of taste when he puts these words into her mouth:

> Yes, great love God knows why . . . Even me . . . But I found a better . . . As I hope you heard . . . Preferable in all respects . . . Kinder . . . Stronger . . . More intelligent . . . Better looking . . . Cleaner . . . Truthful . . . Faithful . . . Sane . . . Yes . . .   (*Eh Joe*, p. 19)

If this were two-edged (as it would be in *Play*) it would work, but it is seriously intended. Not only is this an error of tact, it's a tactical error, since the watcher would normally expect this speaker to be the centre of the ensuing action. By the time he has recovered his bearings, the point is lost. There is a poignant recovery in the closing half-whispered words, of which only a few ('imagine . . . stones . . . lips . . . solitaire . . . eyes . . . breasts . . . hands . . .') are clearly audible, but even this is something of a trick, since the reader of the printed play is able to follow a sequence of thought which the television viewer can only guess at.

Perhaps the relative weakness of *Eh Joe* within the canon is simply that it is *too* simple. Beckett's drama thrives on symbols of unassignable value. 'Who is Godot?' is a meaningful question, but an unanswerable one; 'Did Mr Rooney throw the child out of the train?' is, like 'What worries Bolton?', a problem that has no ready solution, not even for the author. There is no such central perplexity at the heart of *Eh Joe*. The same applies to *Words and Music*, the weakest of the radio plays, in which once again an old man exposes his hunger for the 'balm' of words. Croak keeps two slaves, Words and Music, whom he forces to perform nightly on themes that he hopes will bring him comfort, such as 'love', 'age' and 'the face'. The two minions are in conflict, Words' poetry and Music's melody clash horribly, and after some meagre aesthetic fare Croak shuffles away down the tower steps. A transparent play, this, touching on familiar concerns: the hopelessness of love, the impotence of narrative to soothe wounds, and the ever-cheated indulgence in language which can only offer naked and ultimately unsatisfying verse statements like this:

> Age is when to a man
> Huddled o'er the ingle
> Shivering for the hag
> To put the pan in the bed
> And bring the toddy
> She comes in the ashes
> Who loved could not be won
> Or won not loved
> Or some other trouble
> Comes in the ashes
> Like in that old light
> The face in the ashes
> That old starlight
> On the earth again.   (*Words and Music*, p. 32)

Croak is an impotent impresario, like Opener in *Cascando*, except that Opener's voices are in his head. *Cascando* is an extraordinary dramatization of the central problem of *The Unnamable* (the anguish of the story that can never get told and leave the teller at rest): a meditation on the relationship between the literary artist and his medium, words, using the devices of radio limpidly and explicitly to probe the nature of the creator and of his material, prose narrative. In *Cascando*, Voice is no longer in conflict with Music: they 'link arms', so

that 'from one world to another, it's as though they drew together' (p. 44) in a doomed attempt to pin down Woburn, who
is the subject of Voice's story, and a figure curiously similar
to others in the canon, like O in *Film*, or Macmann whom
Malone runs to ground 'in the heart of the town' (*Three Novels*,
p. 227). The apparently abstract problem of the artist's hope-
lessly mingled dread of – and fascination with – his medium
('I'm afraid to open ... But I must open', p. 46) receives powerful treatment in this, Beckett's last radio play. It has, in
common with the three others I have grouped together,
an intriguing concern not merely with media but also with
message. The parallels are striking: words and story are central
to them all. Considered globally, they reveal an uncommon
preoccupation with the hectoring voice in the mind, the subordinate anima which insists on asserting its independence and
subverting the persona – or, as Beckett himself once put it,
so much more poignantly, in *Text for Nothing XIII*: 'the
screaming silence of no's knife in yes's wound'.

8

Blaze of Hellish Light

HAPPY DAYS (1961)

The title is whimsically ironical, like much else in the play:
'Oh this is going to be another happy day!' Winnie exclaims
early in the action. Aged about fifty, she's a fading but still
well-preserved beauty accompanied by Willie, a decrepit man
in his sixties. Like other Beckettian couples – Pozzo and
Lucky, Hamm and Clov – they have been together a long

time, and they play on each other's weakness and nostalgia. Although Winnie differs from most of the previous protagonists by her female sex, she resembles them in her decaying intellectuality: her consciousness is stocked with the debris of extensive learning, and she quotes fragmentarily but appropriately from such assorted masterpieces as *Cymbeline* ('Fear no more the heat o' the sun', p. 21), *Paradise Lost*, Gray's 'Ode on a Distant Prospect of Eton College' and Fitzgerald's *Omar Khayyám*. Also like some of the others, she reveals an impressive familiarity with the idiosyncrasies of French idiom when she hestitates over whether to refer to hair (*les cheveux*) as 'them' or 'it' (p. 19). And in common with every other character in the canon, she relies extensively on her memories to enable her to talk, and so 'break the silence' (of which, as we know from *Molloy*, the universe is made) that threatens her existence. Her chief dread in fact is that words will fail her: 'I can do no more. Say no more. But I must say more,' she exclaims (p. 44); for just like the two men in *Godot*, she is bailing out the silence in a frantic bid to prevent it sinking her:

> Ah yes, so little to say, so little to do, and the fear so great, certain days, of finding oneself . . . left, with hours still to run, before the bell for sleep, and nothing more to say, nothing more to do, that the days go by, certain days go by, quite by, the bell goes, and little or nothing said, little or nothing done. That is the danger. (*Happy Days*, p. 27)

– which almost has the finality of Hamlet's 'That is the question'. So she resorts, like Hamm, to story-telling, in this case the burlesque tale of how little Mildred was deflowered by a mouse, or the grotesque account of the couple happening to pass by who paused to gawp at her: 'What's the idea? he says – stuck up to her diddies in the bleeding ground – coarse fellow . . . usual drivel' (p. 32). Understandably enough her golden rule is to make a little go a long way so as not to dry up before the closing bell: 'don't squander all your words for the day' (p. 31) is something she needs continually to bear in mind.

Not surprisingly, perhaps, in the scandalous circumstances of her semi-burial, Winnie cannot bear to be alone or 'prattle away with not a soul to hear' (p. 18), but as long as she has Willie with her she does not have to learn to talk to herself. In the first Act only the back of Willie's head and his hands are seen, but in the second he comes round to the front of the stage; in the first Act, however, he is heard to speak quite frequently, whereas in the second he is virtually mute. Winnie remains the only real talker in the play: just as Hamm cannot stand or Clov sit, Winnie cannot move and Willie, who is able to crawl, is the reverse of loquacious: 'Oh I know you were never one to talk,' his companion wittily complains, 'I worship you Winnie be mine and then nothing from that day forth only titbits from *Reynolds' News*' (p. 46). The two (as so often) complement each other through their defects.

Complementarity in characterization and austere symmetry of décor is mirrored in the structure of the play, the first since *Godot* to be written in two Acts, though the second is apt to seem, as *Godot*'s never does, somewhat redundant. The first Act shows Winnie buried up to the waist in the centre of a low mound in a strikingly abstract set devised 'to represent unbroken plain and sky receding to meet in far distance' under a cascade of 'blazing light' (p. 9). In the second Act, the sterile mound (for 'what a blessing nothing grows', p. 27) comes up to Winnie's chin and prevents all local movements except those of her eyes. Willie lies on the ground behind her, hidden for the most part by the mound. The play (which, like all of Beckett's, is meant to be *perceived*) exploits these restrictions to the full: in the first Act Winnie can still busy herself in such feminine chores as painting her lips and adjusting her 'small ornate brimless hat'. In the second Act, however, her actress is faced with the challenge of performing only with the eyes (no wonder this role has attracted artists like Madeleine

Renaud). For in this play, even more than in most of Beckett's, great stress is laid on mime as a form of expression: when Winnie feels she's run out of things to say she decides to 'do' something, and this in turn gives her something to talk about. Rarely indeed has such a commonplace action as teeth-brushing provided so much scope for activity and speech. When Winnie scrubs hers, she not only stretches this out, it provides her with the opportunity of hailing Willie when she turns aside to spit, and the toothbrush enables her to fill many minutes deciphering with the aid of her spectacles the inscription on its handle ('fully guaranteed genuine pure hog's setae'). This discovery, in its turn, elicits from Willie the information that a hog is a 'castrated male swine'. With touching comicality typical of the character and of the entire play, Winnie enthuses joyfully that 'provided one takes the pains' (p. 16), hardly a day goes by without some addition to one's knowledge, however trifling, the addition that is (she pedantically adds).

But as we might expect, the second Act is both shorter and more desperate than the first. A reduced repertoire of comments and actions is repeated: the story of the inquisitive couple, for instance, comes up again. Mysteriously, the parasol, which had dramatically exploded earlier on in the play, is seen back again as Winnie had said it would be, but she no longer has her hands free to open it. The tube of toothpaste, the bottle of pick-me-up mixture, the lipstick that, like Willie's Vaseline which he 'rubs in well' to protect himself from sunburn, were already running out in the first Act; in the second they are an irrelevance. In the second, too, Winnie no longer says her prayers, and not simply because she can no longer clasp her hands: the presence she had felt watching her has now unambiguously revealed itself as the maleficent deity which torments all Beckett's people and is responsible here, no doubt, for a particularly cruel, piercing bell, which reminds us of the prodding goad in *Act Without Words II*.

This bell commands her to 'begin her day' and end it, at prearranged intervals termed 'days' in deference merely to the 'sweet old style' (for the *dolce stil nuovo* is not the only Dantesque note struck in this infernal universe). Little wonder, then, that despite Winnie's brave cheerfulness, 'sorrow keeps breaking in' (p. 27).

At the end of the play Willie, who has mostly spent his time in reading (and occasionally quoting from) the newspaper, and in looking at obscene postcards, appears in full view of the audience, 'dressed to kill'. He makes agonizing efforts to crawl towards Winnie, perhaps in order to kiss her. He fails, but it seems enough to make this a 'happy day' for her, in spite of all. She ends by singing the sentimental waltz from *The Merry Widow*. She shuts her eyes, perhaps to weep, but the vigilant bell jerks her back to reality: her 'day' not yet over, she has to carry on as the curtain falls.

As in other plays, Beckett is concerned here partly to examine the essential human bond, one of mingled tenderness and loathing, and view it free from distracting elements, like sexual concupiscence ('sadness after intimate sexual intercourse one is familiar with of course', remarks Winnie knowingly). Strong emotions, as in *Krapp's Last Tape*, are only distant memories ('that day,' she muses, 'the lake . . . the reeds', p. 39), or they're the subject of bawdy puns, like 'formication' (p. 24). The starkness of the present situation is underlined by the barrenness of the décor; and the complex counterpointing of the dramaturgy, in which elements weave in and out, repeated and refracted continually throughout the play, stands in sharp contrast. For in the later works, Beckett's themes become simpler as his technique grows more complex: I am reminded of an analogy with a piece of music written about the same time as *Happy Days*, just as stark in its manner but equally demanding on its performers: Penderecki's *Threnody for the Victims of Hiroshima*. Beckett would probably not find the analogy far-fetched; for when the 'words fail . . .

must fail' (pp. 20, 25), the only appropriate lament is the hard gaze that ends this play, or chords almost as abrasive as Winnie's bell.

9

The Net Closes

PLAY (1963)

In 1902, in the Imperial Institute, South Kensington, Edward Gordon Craig produced *Bethlehem*, a nativity play by Laurence Housman. The last scene is described by Denis Bablet as follows:

> The stage was arranged as an amphitheatre, with the shepherds grouped around the Virgin and the crib. When Mary drew the coverings from the cradle, there was no doll inside to represent the Child, but light streamed up from its depths into the faces of those gathered round it. The divine presence was indicated by the radiant faces of the shepherds gazing at the Child. Light had never before been used like this in a performance.   (*Edward Gordon Craig*, p. 54)

How would this scene have affected the members of its audience? They would have received, I think, a double impression: their sense of their own insignificance and uncertainty as they sat in darkness in their seats would have been first emphasized by and then blended with their sense of the power and glory of the light and of the certainty on the faces of the characters exposed to it. They would have taken part in a theatrical experience equivalent to St Paul's famous sentence in I Corinthians: 'For now we see through a glass, darkly; but then face to face; now I know in part; but then I know even as also I am known.'

Beckett's *Play* – written in English but first performed in Germany – uses Craig's light to produce an opposite effect. The light in *Play*, situated now 'at the centre of the footlights', plays over the faces of the three characters on the stage one at a time, switching on and switching off speech exactly as a playwright does when he moves from one line of dialogue on his page to the next. The light itself is sometimes faint, sometimes brighter, and Hugh Kenner has noted that:

> In directing the 1964 London and Paris performances, Beckett virtually improvised a new work (*Play no. 2?*) by modifying the rigour of the light. It grew tired; it faded (and the voices with it); it relaxed its rigorous sequence for soliciting speeches. Perhaps it would eventually go out and release the players into non-being; or perhaps it was teasing them with this hope. When he prepared the French text for publication (*Comédie*, 1966), Beckett did not however incorporate these revisions, though he outlined them in a note as an alternative mode of performance.

Jean-Marie Serreau has recorded that Beckett insisted, at rehearsals for the French production, on the light being operated by hand, so that it should come from a 'more human' source. But whether or not the light itself fades or wavers, its impotence as interrogator, author or conductor is sufficiently revealed by its failure to elicit from its three 'victims' anything beyond scraps of invincible ignorance, encrusted in cliché and uttered in toneless voices from expressionless faces. This light does not so much animate the characters on stage as drain them, so that the darkness which surrounds them becomes by contrast a source almost of strength and comfort, just as the audience seated in its own darkness is brought to feel a surprising sense of its own adequacy, its comparative significance and certainty. From this point of view, the theatrical effect of the light in *Play* is somewhat similar to the experience of visiting a graveyard – the visitor is made keenly aware of his own flesh and blood by comparison with the lack of it all around him.

The three characters are, after all, for the most part funeral urns. Even their faces are 'so lost to age and aspect as to seem almost part of urns'. Physically they recall *The Unnamable*'s character Mahood, who lived, or imagined himself living, in a jar outside a restaurant, his protruding head illuminated with lanterns, facing a slaughterhouse. Their plight owes something perhaps to that of Pope Nicholas III in the nineteenth canto of the *Inferno* whom Dante – crueller and more certain of his ground than Beckett – found wedged upside down in a hole in the rock, with flames playing on his feet. What they suffer, however, is neither quite torment nor quite purgation; they are nearer to a triple version of Dante's Belacqua who had to wait in Ante-Purgatory for the whole span of his life to unfold again before he could move upwards into Purgatory, with the difference that the characters in *Play*, sharing Belacqua's embalmed present and his imprisonment in the past, have no change to look forward to in the future, or are aware of none.

Their past, though, is of a very peculiar kind; or rather, in the manner of clues in detective stories, it is so very unpeculiar as to draw particular attention to itself. The audience, confronted initially with a blatant *memento mori*, subjected immediately afterwards to a 'faint' and 'largely unintelligible' babble of voices (a chorus at cross-purposes), has scarcely settled itself lugubriously into its seats with every expectation of further bafflement and alienation, when it begins to receive familiar signals, winks and beckonings, from the text: 'I said to him, Give her up. I swore by all I held most sacred –' from the first urn with a female voice; 'One morning as I was sitting stitching by the open window she burst in and flew at me' from the second female urn; 'We were not long together when she smelled the rat. Give up that whore, she said . . .' from the urn in the middle with a male voice. Just as the members of

Craig's audience would have felt instantly at home with a New Testament scene whose content and characters they had known intimately since childhood, so the members of Beckett's audience can hardly feel less so to discover that what they took to be urns turn out to be just Him, Her and the Other Woman in disguise.

Not that this fragmentary recital of middle-class adultery, told in the past tense in passionless voices by characters unaware of each other's presence on stage, without names and with only the most rudimentary 'characteristics' – the man hiccups, the wife is bossy, the other woman has a wild laugh – is lifelike, far from it, it is a tissue of the second-hand, the pre-digested and the pre-packaged. In a word, it is theatrical. An audience of regular theatregoers – or for that matter of cinemagoers, television-watchers, readers of novels or newspapers – cannot help but respond automatically to this talk of butlers, lawn-mowers, 'bloodhounds', Rivieras, morning rooms, vanity-bags, as to comfortable and homely furniture; cannot help but relax in the friendly warmth of such phrases as 'settle my hash', 'professional commitments', 'I bear you no ill-feeling', 'on the way back by Ash and Snodland'.

But once this section is over, once the characters and their situation have been set in their familiar grooves, the text again grows disconcerting. The characters continue from time to time to regurgitate gobbets of their past, the two women still scoring off one another in retrospect, the man seeming to have arrived at a new sense of detachment ('I know now, all that was just . . . play'), but it becomes alarmingly evident that they do not know where they are or what has become of them or what the light wants with them. Indeed the audience now knows more than they do and as much as the light, that is to say that there are three characters on the stage, not one. And the section closes with a clinching revelation of the characters' ignorance and the audience's superior knowledge, when the man says: 'Am I as much as . . . being seen?'

In his study of Proust, Beckett speaks of 'the beautiful convention of the "da capo" as a testimony to the intimate and ineffable nature of an art that is perfectly intelligible and perfectly inexplicable' (*Proust*, p. 92). He has often made use of the convention himself, notably at the beginning of the second Act of *Waiting for Godot* in Vladimir's shaggy-dog song, but never with such wholehearted relish as on the last page of *Play* with the laconic stage direction: 'Repeat play exactly'. What is the result? Everything on the stage returns exactly as it was before: the urns, the actors, the light, the darkness, the text and the intervals in the text, though in a note in the later edition of *Play*, Beckett suggests certain small variations in the intensity of the light, the breathlessness of the voices and the order of the speeches. But everything has a different effect for the audience, not as if it were a different audience on another night of *Play*'s run, but as if the audience had come closer to being the author. The characters' ignorance which was revealed in the later section of the play now hangs about like a damp mist among the comparative certainties of the earlier section; the second-hand adultery now becomes doubly second-hand; the passages of text which might have seemed first time round to be abridgements of experience, tips of icebergs, are now seen to be all that there is or was, with nothing underneath them; the light is seen to be working to a prearranged and unalterable plot; the characters not characters but actors who have conned their lines and the way to say them by rote and could as soon embellish them as parrots. All this the people in the audience took for granted when they first entered the theatre for the purpose of seeing a play, but they are now made consciously aware of it, they are made to take account of it. If they came in with their minds focused on getting out again, after a suitable dénouement to the play, they must now re-focus on the play itself, on the patterns of sight and sound prepared for them by the author and his actors, with or without dénouement.

And now it becomes clear that the patterns, the action of *Play* itself on stage, form an image of the theatrical experience in which the audience is taking part. The light and the characters – author, actors and audience for the purposes of the image – present first the play, the little reach-me-down adultery, and then their consciousness of it and themselves in the present, the intelligible followed by the inexplicable. But by repeating it, they cause the inexplicable to seep into the intelligible and the intelligible into the inexplicable, just as the sense of identity which the individuals in the audience brought with them into the theatre from outside is being constantly diluted with their experiences inside. And once this process has been set in motion, the action on stage reflecting the experience it gives rise to in the audience, the audience's experience reflecting back the action on stage, the almost impossible is achieved: the audience, instead of simply witnessing and reacting to patterns of sight and sound placed at some remove, is drawn into them. Where, on Mr Endon's chessboard, his own black pieces danced while Murphy's white ones staggered and dithered, where in *Waiting for Godot* Lucky performed 'The Net' while the rest of the actors and the audience merely looked on, here in *Play* the whole board capers, actors and audience together enter 'The Net'.

Play is, to date, the most perfect example of Beckett's dramatic art, the most self-contained, the most exacting and self-exacting. What he said of Joyce's *Work in Progress* in 1929 he has at last fully brought about in the theatre (hence, of course, *Play*'s title): it 'is not *about* something; *it is that something itself*'. This is one of the most noticeable things in Beckett – and perhaps partly accounts for the way he attracts commentators like moths – that what he said in his earliest work he has more and more specifically done, that his essays, poems, stories, novels and plays have been from the beginning like a single rocket launched at a distant target, its course sustained over a period of forty years, its aim corrected with narrower and narrower adjustments to hit the mark. The passage in Beckett's study of Proust, for example, in which he sums up the conclusion of *A la recherche du temps perdu*, seems to preconceive *Play* from a distance of thirty-three years:

> The most trivial experience – he [Proust] says in effect – is encrusted with elements that logically are not related to it and have consequently been rejected by our intelligence: it is imprisoned in a vase filled with a certain perfume . . . and raised to a certain temperature. These vases are suspended along the height of our years, and, not being accessible to our intelligent memory, are in a sense immune, the purity of their climatic content is guaranteed by forgetfulness, each one is kept at its distance, at its date. So that when the imprisoned microcosm is besieged in the manner described [that is, by accident, through the action of involuntary memory], we are flooded by a new air and a new perfume (new precisely because already experienced), and we breathe the true air of Paradise, of the only Paradise that is not the dream of a madman, the Paradise that has been lost.
>
> (*Proust*, pp. 73–4)

The trivial experiences are there in *Play*, to be sure, imprisoned in their vases and even encrusted with unrelated elements:

> м. When I saw her again she knew. She was looking – (*hiccup*) – wretched. Pardon. Some fool was cutting grass. A little rush, then another. The problem was how to convince her that no . . . revival of intimacy was involved. (*Play*, p. 13)

But where is the air of Paradise? Certainly not in the stale and deliberate formulas from their past which the characters dredge up at the light's insistence; still less in their nervy ignorance about their present state. But the curious thing is that, returning through the play a second time, we do breathe it, we catch it not *in* the repeated formulas but as it were *near* them, as though the words themselves excluded it but at the same time contained it, as though the talking heads acted like stoppers to the contents of the vases. The strange crystallized rhythms of the text, its absurd period flavour, seem to trace

Get up & go

E & OE, two taxmen.

E: *Irish, acidulated, vindictive.*

OE: *British, acidulated, vindictive.*

(Part of an advertisement put out by the Industrial Development Authority of Ireland)

the outline of what has been forgotten, of what has been left out by the deliberate memory:

> w1. Judge then of my astoundment when one fine morning, as I was sitting stricken in the morning room, he slunk in, fell on his knees before me, buried his face in my lap and . . confessed.
>   (*Play*, p. 11)

The wife is offering us a spotlit attitude, a posture of certainty and competence which she adopted at the time and which she cannot whenever she speaks shake off; the character, pressed into service by its author, must utter words in more or less common, therefore more or less starched, use; but along the edges of the wife's attitude, suggested directly to the subconscious by the way the character's words spring at each other or fall apart, are stored up the darkness and silence in which she did lose something, in which the character failed to express a meaning, and in which we, since *Play* is a work of art designed for that purpose, may intimately experience, ineffably regain the loss.

10

Into Action

ACT WITHOUT WORDS I (1956), ACT WITHOUT WORDS II (1958), FILM (1964), COME AND GO (1965), BREATH (1969)

Beckett is, above all, a master of dramatic speech. In the course of renewing the theatrical experience as a whole, he has restored to the words spoken on a stage – traditionally the dominant element in a theatrical experience – the self-sufficiency, the sculptural quality of poetry. Any modern playwright who wants his plays to *be* something rather than to be *about* something must inevitably confront this obstacle: that the words he uses are in common coinage and automatically convey established meanings; meanings, that is to say, which are either straightforward pieces of information without association ('she went out at five o'clock') or whose associations have become stock ('blood is thicker than water'). When Beckett turned to writing in French it was no doubt partly to escape the particularly dense mass of stock association with which the English language is burdened. T. S. Eliot and Christopher Fry both made determined attempts to restore 'poetry' to the English stage, but they seem to have misunderstood the nature of the difficulty; at any rate they merely heightened and decorated the surface manner in which their characters communicated without achieving any substantial change in *what* they communicated. Curiously enough, Eliot himself had already done for verse what he failed to do for the theatre and what Beckett must have learnt as much from *The Waste Land* as from anywhere else. For where Joyce took the more obvious course of jerking the English language to its feet and making it take part in orgies, Eliot, with more subtlety, made it lie down and die. And this was what Beckett had clearly learnt by the time he returned to English with his own translation of *Waiting for Godot*: that words could be rescued from their subservience to a single meaning – the prosaic flatness of naturalism – or to a stock association – the straitjacket of cliché – if they ceased pretending to be vehicles of communication between the characters.

Beckett's plays deliberately draw attention to the inability of the characters' words to communicate a meaning or to pass information – except what is so stale and habitual as to be ludicrous – with the result that familiar words and phrases appear in a new light: partly as sounds and rhythms for their own sake, partly as archaic, petrified 'meanings' which have been deserted by their context. And just as Ozymandias, in Shelley's poem, by being reduced to 'two vast and trunkless legs of stone' becomes more fraught with possibility, more stirring to the imagination, more memorable than he was as a mere King of Kings, so Lucky's tattered theology, Hamm's 'we're getting on', the man in *Play*'s 'Personally I always preferred Lipton's' continue to inhabit and tease the mind with the persistence of objects whose original purpose has been forgotten or become obsolete and whose present existence is therefore strictly 'meaningless'.

We have seen how in *Play* – more accurately than in any of his previous plays – Beckett made these impotent, stultified words and phrases express their own inadequacy, trace the outlines of silence and loss. In the so-called 'dramaticule' *Come and Go* he uses only 121 words to achieve the same effect. Three women, shadows of the three *bourgeois* mastodons of *Eleuthéria*, almost identical as to their coats, hats and even faces (concealed beneath the brims of their hats), sit on a scarcely visible bench surrounded with darkness; each in turn leaves the pool of light briefly, when the other two share an inaudible confidence which causes them to gasp and show pity for the absent party. The compression is virtuoso – Jean-Louis Barrault has compared the piece to a sonata by Webern – when one considers that in less words than I have so far used in this paragraph Beckett contrives to give us the complete history of three little girls from school who have grown old without being married and who are about to die. He does it by inducing the silence to work for him, as a Chinese painter makes a few brush-strokes create a landscape out of areas of white paper. In a single line – 'Just sit together as we used to, in the playground at Miss Wade's' – Beckett delineates the characters' distant past, brushes in their present and by making the two work on each other persuades us to imagine the time between. But *Come and Go* is not simply a repetition in miniature of the effect of *Play*, for being set in life rather than limbo it contains two kinds of silence: silence apropos of the past and silence apropos of the future. The three characters join hands as in a children's game, the whole piece proceeds with the gravity, formality and brevity of a children's game, but the game is as it were a frame or fence round those three inaudible confidences, obscure wells into which each character in turn falls dragging one third of the rickety fence after her.

Nevertheless, it is doubtful whether *Come and Go* would make such a strong effect if it stood on its own, if it were not hoisted on the shoulders of the earlier and larger works. One cannot be certain how it would do if one did not know it was by Beckett, if one were not already aware of the full power of his theatrical voice elsewhere. When that voice is entirely absent, as it is in *Breath*, the two *Acts Without Words* and *Film*, what is left is decidedly too little.

The silence in *Breath* lasts five seconds and is framed on the near side by a baby's first cry, an inspiration of breath and an increase of light which together last ten seconds; and on the far side by a decrease of light, an expiration of breath and the same baby's cry which again last ten seconds. The stage is occupied by a litter of 'miscellaneous rubbish' which is given a five-second prologue and a five-second epilogue under a faint light. The play is, as John Calder has pointed out in his introduction to the published 'text', a speechless demonstration of Pozzo's words in *Waiting for Godot*: 'They give birth astride of a grave, the light gleams an instant, then it's night once more.' One cannot say that it improves on them and since *Breath* takes twice as long to perform, it smacks less of the economy for which Calder esteems it than of otiosity. However, since it was originally sent on a postcard to Kenneth Tynan for his erotic revue *Oh! Calcutta*, it is perhaps better taken as a joke, to which Tynan wittily riposted by including naked people among the miscellaneous rubbish.

The two *Acts Without Words* seem to be loosely based on

punishments from the classical underworld: the first on that of Tantalus, who was condemned to stand in a stream which receded whenever he bent down to drink, while fruit-laden branches overhead whisked out of his reach; the second that of Sisyphus who had to trudge up a hill pushing a boulder which fell to the bottom every time he reached the top. The first *Act Without Words* uses a single actor and a variety of stage machinery and props which are set against him by malevolent persons unknown off stage, the whole mime recalling the passage in *Waiting for Godot* where Vladimir and Estragon contemplate hanging themselves from a bough of their tree. But *Act Without Words I* is by comparison overexplicit, over-emphasized and even, unless redeemed by its performer, so unparticularized as to verge on the banal.

Act Without Words II is to be played on 'a low and narrow platform at back of stage, violently lit', so as to give the effect of a frieze, an indirect acknowledgement perhaps of the mime's classical origin as well as an early version of the front-stage frieze effect which Beckett used in *Play* and *Come and Go*. The mime's two characters, one sluggish, the other brisk, suggest as Vladimir and Estragon sometimes do, two aspects of a single person; they nibble carrots like Estragon and use toothbrushes like Winnie in *Happy Days*. The goad on wheels which prods them out of their sacks is a more outlandish version of Winnie's bell and the light in *Play*, just as the sacks bridge the gap between *Endgame*'s dustbins and Winnie's mound or the urns in *Play*. Apart from its interest as a rough sketch for the formal technical devices of the later plays, *Act Without Words II* bears as much or as little comparison with Beckett's larger works as the dumb-show in *Hamlet* with *Hamlet* as a whole.

One might have expected that *Film* – short, silent, set in 1929 and performed by one of the great comedians of the silent screen – would have given double satisfaction, that of the music-hall tradition on which Beckett drew for *Waiting for Godot* and that of *Waiting for Godot* itself, the tradition and its strange progeny locked in a strange embrace. In the event, *Film* is unsatisfying on both counts, and though one may criticize Buster Keaton's performance for dullness and Alan Schneider's direction for visual apathy, it is surely the script which they both follow only too faithfully, that is responsible. *Film*'s script is what none of Beckett's other works are, an unfleshed intellectual skeleton. One has only to read Beckett's opening general comments, expressed with uncharacteristic clumsiness, to catch the note of falsity, to realize that he has here committed the sin against his own holy ghost, of putting the concept before the shape, of explaining, of showing what he has explained, of showing no more than what he has explained. Even the reminiscences of his other work – the picture on the wall from *Endgame*, now turned round to show the face of 'God the Father'; the past encapsulated in a packet of photographs; Murphy's rocking-chair – seem more like plagiarisms than reverberations. And the final identification of the camera with Buster Keaton's second self – a memory of Krapp and his *doppelgänger* – is too self-evidently a theatrical device which for once outplays its master, since it forces him to stoop to a conjuring trick.

What is perhaps chiefly wrong with *Film*, as with the other speechless pieces, is that when Beckett ceases to speak he ceases to speak to himself and begins playing charades. It becomes clear that the physical movements, gestures, comic routines which form an accompaniment to the words in all his plays are no more than accompaniment; the real action in Beckett's plays is in the words and between the words.

II

Performance and Response

It all begins, not (as you might expect) with *Waiting for Godot*'s crucial opening on 5 January 1953, but with a college parody staged anonymously long before: between 19 and 21 February 1931, in fact, when the Peacock Theatre in Dublin saw the first (and last) performances of Beckett's earliest dramatic work, *Le Kid*, written in collaboration with a life-long friend, Georges Pelorson, at that time French exchange lecturer at Trinity College, Dublin. All trace of this send-up of Corneille's famous heroic tragedy *Le Cid* seems to have disappeared, except for a laconic review carried a few days later by the student newspaper:

> *Le Kid* . . . made us laugh . . . with a rather bitter laughter, and it was not at Corneille we were laughing. Really wasn't it rather naïve? It reminded us forcibly of those grand old parodies that used to be shown at the Gaiety some forty years past . . . unless you happened to hate Corneille very very heartily it was rather a strain on the digestion . . . We have a theory it was the work of Guy de Maupassant – his very last work, if not, indeed, posthumous. None of the actors [Beckett himself played Don Diègue] was outstanding, but all were capable.
>
> (*T.C.D., A College Miscellany*, 26 February 1931, p. 116)

So much for *Le Kid*; if the manuscript is ever found it might make interesting reading. Certainly the critical reaction to its performance does not differ markedly from others we shall be discussing. The next play, *Eleuthéria*, has of course never been produced, and so we jump more than twenty years to the saga of *Godot*'s staging.

Beckett wrote *En attendant Godot* rapidly, in the winter of 1948–9, between the novels *Malone meurt* and *L'Innommable*, and on this occasion he naturally aimed at something more professional than a college production. It happened, the way these things often do, that at the time Roger Blin, who had been a friend of Antonin Artaud and acted in one of his plays before the war, was putting on Strindberg's *Ghost Sonata* at the Gaîté-Montparnasse theatre, and Beckett went to see it. Thinking that Blin was the ideal person to create his own play, he sent him the typescript. It was not until some time later that Blin actually made his acquaintance; far too shy to face Blin himself, Beckett dealt at first through his wife Suzanne. When they finally met, Blin was curious to know why he had been chosen. Because Blin was faithful to Strindberg, both to the letter and the spirit, and because the theatre was nearly empty, was the answer. Beckett was sure – Blin relates – that his own text would therefore be respected and that the theatre would be empty, which seemed to the author the ideal condition for a good performance.

Undeterred by the eccentricity of this view, Blin was won over by the play. He claims that at first he did not perceive the full import of its theme, but was impressed by the quality of the dialogue and the characterization. Unable to persuade the Gaîté-Montparnasse to take the work (soon afterwards, in any case, the theatre went bankrupt), Blin had to wait three years to put it on. A small official bursary enabled him, early in 1953, to stage the play at Jean-Marie Serreau's Théâtre Babylone (since also defunct). Interestingly enough, the choice of *Godot* itself was largely fortuitous: Blin had also in his hands at the time *Eleuthéria*, but in the end decided against it, mainly because *Godot* required only five characters, whereas *Eleuthéria* demanded over three times that number, and money was short; the greater maturity and profundity of *Godot* was not, at that stage, a major consideration.

It is a depressing reflection on the state of drama even in

such a theatrically rich centre as Paris that it took an immensely gifted director like Blin three years to secure the resources (and then only with the aid of a government subsidy to first plays) and find a theatre (and then only a modest experimental house) to enable him to create what is now universally recognized as one of the classics of post-war literature. However, the difficulties once overcome, the reaction to the play, and to Pierre Latour's performance as Estragon, Lucien Raimbourg's as Vladimir, Jean Martin's as Lucky and Blin's as Pozzo, was – on the part both of critics and audiences – predictably mixed, but on the whole sympathetically favourable. The opinion of *Le Figaro*'s influential theatre reviewer, Jean-Jacques Gautier, was such (Harold Hobson recalled in the *Sunday Times*, 28 April 1963) that he declined to mention it in his collected criticism, and if the equally influential Thierry Maulnier, since elected to the French Academy, conceded in the *Revue de Paris* that the play was not without importance, he none the less dismissed it as a nine-days' wonder. The very first review, by Sylvain Zegel in *La Libération*, more shrewdly prophesied a long life for the play, and did not hesitate to hail Beckett as one of the best contemporary playwrights. But the flotsam and jetsam of such ephemera, for or against, is insignificant beside the permanent value of the reactions of four fellow-writers. Jean Anouilh, in *Arts* for 27 February 1953, did not beat about the bush: the opening of *Godot*, he asserted, was as important as the first staging, in Paris forty years earlier, of a Pirandello play, and he was telling the simple truth – Pirandello's impact on the dramaturgy of the inter-war years was on much the same scale as Beckett's has been in the last couple of decades. To Jacques Audiberti, writing for the same magazine on 16 January, *Godot* appeared 'a perfect work which deserves a triumph', and Armand Salacrou claimed in the same place on 27 February that they had all been waiting 'for this play of our time'. A more extended and reflective account was contributed in February by Alain Robbe-Grillet to *Critique*; if he felt misgivings over Beckett's 'dangerously contagious regression', he still revealed a discriminating enthusiasm for the achievement.

In the course of his review Robbe-Grillet credited Blin with emphasizing the 'circus aspects' of the play and thus contributing materially to its success. Blin is in fact one of the few directors to have influenced Beckett: it was at Blin's instigation that he cut several passages that seemed too long or literary, or that broke the tension in some way. This explains why the second French edition, which appeared after the creation at the Babylone, differs from the first of 1952, and why the English translation, carried out by Beckett himself and published in 1954, shows extensive deletions. A measure of his gratitude to Blin for giving him confidence as a playwright is shown by the dedication of *Endgame* to this his first director, whose basic approach to *Godot* has broadly been accepted as definitive (he was even invited to Germany to produce it there, although he speaks no German). His production was next staged in Paris at the Théâtre Hébertot in 1956; but perhaps the most perfect resurrection was during the season devoted to the 'New Theatre', in Florence and at the Paris Odéon, in May 1961. Giacometti was commissioned to design the décor (a memorably slender tree in an empty landscape), and Blin who, as a tall slim man, had never been happy in the role of Pozzo, entrusted it with success to the burly Jean-Jacques Bourgois. Since then, and always in Blin's charge, *Godot* has established itself as an uncontested classic of the French stage – almost like Racine, remarked Bertrand Poirot-Delpech half-jokingly in *Le Monde* (19 March 1970), it has become 'one of the pillars of our theatre'.

Its fortunes elsewhere in the world have been, if anything, even more brilliant. It was seen in Warsaw, and then it was staged in London (at the Arts Theatre club first, from 3 August 1955). After 12 September it was transferred to the

Criterion Theatre, a few cuts having been made in the text
to satisfy the Lord Chamberlain. It ran there until the following May. This London production was preceded by the
same rather sordid difficulties as the Paris creation had been,
and the New York staging was to be also. The first project
had been for Peter Glenville to direct Alec Guinness in the
role of Vladimir and Ralph Richardson in that of Estragon.
Ralph Richardson has written movingly of his initial enthusiasm for the part being damped by Beckett's failure to
offer any elucidation as to what Pozzo represents: 'I am sadly
literal-minded', he has said, 'and don't like obscurity anywhere' (*Sunday Times*, 10 July 1960), so on finding that
Beckett could not 'explain' the work to him, he let the part
go. But he claimed that the play 'seemed somehow to haunt
me' – even during the time he was playing in Graham Greene's
Complaisant Lover! In this he was quite unlike John Gielgud,
who when later approached about *Endgame* turned it down
because he 'couldn't stand it or understand it', any more than
he could tolerate *Godot*, of which he said: 'when I saw it, I
had practically to be chained to my seat' (*Sunday Times*, 24
September 1961). In fact, apart from Bert Lahr, America's
Estragon, and Madeleine Renaud the French Winnie, few
prominent stars or famous performers have managed to
accommodate their style to Beckett's plays: these have, on the
whole, been much better served by initially less well known
but more flexible actors, like Jack MacGowran or Jean
Martin. Such men, in common with the directors for whom
they work, are able to accept that a play may have a mythical
significance which cannot be summed up in a few sentences
and which, in any case, only emerges in a performance that
seeks as faithfully as possible to follow the author's instruc-
tions and leave the overtones to look after themselves. It was
probably better for the play, in fact, that Richardson did
not in the end take the part of Estragon: he would undoubtedly have given a fine performance, but it would have been

very much a *performance*, not unlike that offered by Madeleine Renaud as Winnie, rather than the more effective playing of, say, Alfred Lynch, who was all the more eloquent in the part in 1964 because he was self-effacing, and allowed the character to come alive through him.

Before *Waiting for Godot* eventually fell in the way of the young man who was to be its first British director, Peter Hall, the Earl of Harewood wished to produce it, but had to give up the idea through lack of funds. But at last it went into rehearsal, and Peter Bull (Pozzo) has amusingly described the experience as 'the most gruelling that I've ever experienced in all my puff' (*I Know the Face, but . . .*, London, 1959): his bald wig caused him acute discomfort, the props he was required to carry kept getting in the way, and since so many of the cues were identical 'it was remarkably easy to leave out whole chunks of the play'. The daily papers treated the first night with bafflement or derision, but the following Sunday Harold Hobson published one of the most moving and perceptive notices of his career in the play's defence, and the equally influential Kenneth Tynan testified to the way it 'pricked and stimulated' his nervous system. This turned the tide, and *Godot* has never failed to attract British audiences ever since. Nevertheless, it is now recognized that Peter Hall's production was not perfect: it overstressed the tramps aspect, and went beyond Beckett's indications for décor by adding a dustbin and miscellaneous rubbish to the required tree.

Early in 1956 Faber and Faber, who had managed to secure the English publication rights in spite of initial hesitations, published the expurgated version acted at the Criterion (the full text was not to be published or performed until nearly ten years later). This was reviewed in the *Times Literary Supplement* by an anonymous critic later identified as G. S. Fraser, who claimed that the play 'extracts from the *idea* of boredom the most genuine pathos and enchanting comedy'. He went on to remark that it is 'essentially a prolonged and sustained metaphor about the nature of human life', and this unassuming exegesis triggered off a correspondence with the editor about the 'meaning' of the play which continued for several weeks and in which William Empson, among others, took part. After six letters from his readers the editor terminated this very British exchange by singling out, for especial praise amongst those submitted to him, an interpretation to the effect that Vladimir represents the soul, Estragon the body, and Pozzo and Lucky damnation; and he expressed the hope that the author himself would write to the paper and clear up the mystery. Needless to say, Beckett did no such thing, which is perhaps not so surprising in view of the discovery (made by one of his fictional characters, Molloy) that the *Times Literary Supplement* serves admirably as a makeshift blanket since 'even farts made no impression on its never-failing toughness and impermeability' (*Three Novels*, p. 30).

London's next major production of *Waiting for Godot*, Alan Simpson's with an Irish cast from Dublin, prompted Raymond Williams, reviewing it in the *New Statesman* for 19 May 1961, to stress Beckett's 'very powerful dramatic imagery, of a virtually universal kind'. With characteristic perceptiveness, Williams took the opportunity to draw attention to the play's basic, 'quite formal' structure, and to the fact that 'because of its flexibility and subtlety, even its deep ambiguity of tone, it is a play that requires an emotionally educated audience'. The British Broadcasting Corporation, which had already done something to educate that audience with *All That Fall* in 1957, continued the good work by broadcasting *Godot* on television in 1961 and on sound radio as part of a series called 'From the Fifties' in 1962. When the play was revived at the Royal Court Theatre late in 1964 there was little difficulty about the audience, which 'clapped and clapped and went on clapping', according to the *Daily*

Telegraph reviewer. This production of the definitive text by Anthony Page, supervised by Beckett, had the kind of authoritativeness shown by the Paris Odéon staging of 1961. The press this time was uniformly favourable. 'I admit it', confessed Bernard Levin in the *Daily Mail*, 'Mr Hobson was right': not all the word-eating was as candid as this, but in general the tenor was the same. Reviewers even wondered what all the fuss had been about nine years previously: the play, they roundly asserted, wasn't in the least obscure, but had the limpid simplicity of a great classic. On the eve of opening the *Daily Mail* permitted itself a jocularly seasonal note: 'a stone's throw from the citadels of panto, Lucky makes his bow . . . but it's a far cry from Mother Goose'; for no longer was anyone afraid of the big bad wolf. With characteristic modesty Harold Hobson did not waste space on I-told-you-so's, but he did just allow himself an aside: '*Waiting for Godot* – we all know it now – is a very great play', he murmured in the *Sunday Times* of 17 January 1965. For the rest of his notice he bestowed glowing (and fully merited) praise on Nicol Williamson's performance as Vladimir and 'his jaunty Scots accent, his sudden bursts of gaiety, his agilely shambling half-run, half-walk, his confident assertions followed immediately by doubts and qualifications, his innumerable suggestions for games and diversions, his brief but total collapses'. In such moments Williamson stood 'absolutely forlorn in broken bowler and ragged trousers, nothing moving except his sad, distressed eyes . . .' Jack MacGowran's equally impressive Lucky was praised by Ronald Bryden in the *New Statesman* (8 January 1965): 'MacGowran has acted himself so far into Beckett's mind he almost seems part of its imagery.' So well did he (like Paul Curran as Pozzo and Alfred Lynch as Estragon) serve their roles, that a newcomer to the play might have been forgiven for assuming it had been written specially for them. They achieved the difficult feat of clearly differentiating the characters: Estragon came over suitably 'morose', Pozzo 'hectoring', Lucky 'doleful' and Vladimir 'restless', to quote some of the laudatory epithets employed by reviewers.

There have, of course, been other memorable productions in the British Isles: in December 1967 the Traverse Theatre in Edinburgh sought to remind its audience of those citizens 'who will toast Christmas with surgical spirit' by choosing as the main prop a dead Christmas tree without foliage, and Peter O'Toole not long ago gave a fine performance as Vladimir at the Abbey Theatre in Dublin. Enterprising producers have sought to give an original twist to the universality of the plot by, for example, employing an all-Negro cast (Broadway, January 1957) or playing successfully before a penitentiary audience (San Quentin, California, November 1957). But these last two American productions had had the way prepared for them the previous year at Miami, Florida, by Alan Schneider's agony and ecstasy.

Schneider, born in Kharkov during the Russian Revolution and brought to the United States by his parents in 1923, came to the theatre (like another fine director, Jean-Marie Serreau), after embarking on a quite different career: in Serreau's case it was architecture, in Schneider's physics. That he has earned the confidence and respect of three very different playwrights (Albee, Beckett and Pinter), to the extent of becoming their official American interpreter, is a measure of his importance in New York theatrical life. But the beginnings (amusingly recounted in a 'Personal Chronicle' in the *Chelsea Review* for September 1958) were far more difficult than the satisfactory present situation would lead one to believe. The cosmopolitan Schneider heard about an exciting new play called *En attendant Godot* from a friend in Zurich in time to get to see the original Babylone production in Paris, and from that point onwards looked out for an opportunity to direct the play in the United States, despite the doubts of agents and producers (shared to some extent

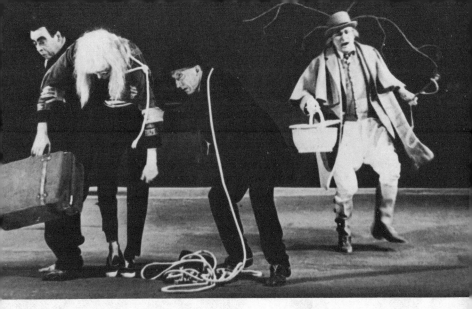

1a *En Attendant Godot*, Paris, 1953

1b *Waiting for Godot*, London, 1964

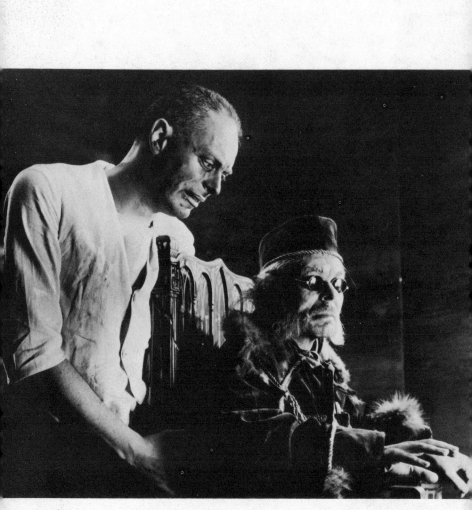

2 *Fin de Partie*, London, 1957

Endgame, London, 1964

Das letzte Band (Krapp's Last Tape), Berlin, 1969

Act Without Words I, London, 1962

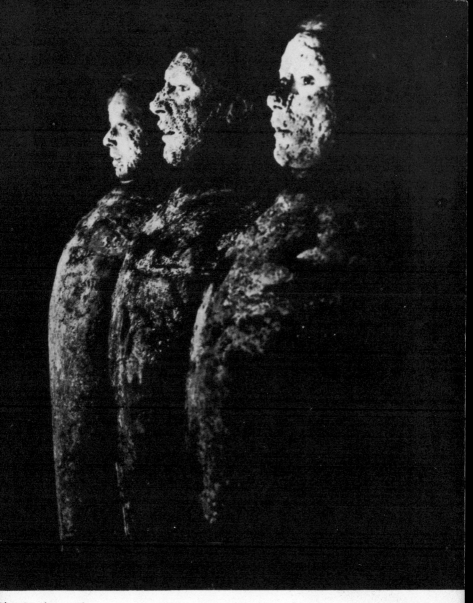

Play, London, 1964

(at left) *Happy Days*, New York, 1961

8a *Come and Go*, Berlin, 1965

8b Samuel Beckett with the tramps from *Waiting for Godot*

by Schneider himself) that the play was not a commercial proposition in the American context. Eventually, on Thornton Wilder's recommendation, the producer Michael Myerberg, who had already signed Bert Lahr for the part of Estragon and Tom Ewell as Vladimir, offered him the direction, which he at once accepted. Myerberg sent him to Paris to talk to Beckett (this was the start of a close friendship), and on to London to see the Criterion production. He had the rare experience, in the company of the author incognito, of attending every performance for a week and getting the benefit of his reactions: 'My fondest memories', Schneider recalls, 'are of Sam's clutching my arm from time to time and in a clearly-heard stage whisper saying: "It's ahl wrahng! He's doing it ahl wrahng!"' Thus primed, he returned to put the play into rehearsal, but the manager made a cardinal error in deciding on Miami for the pre-Broadway try-out. It was, Schneider admits, 'a spectacular flop': he had feared the worst when he arrived in Miami in January 1956 to discover that the wealthy vacationers were being invited by the advance publicity to enjoy 'the laugh sensation of two continents'. Things picked up a little when disappointed holidaymakers gave way to audiences of students and young people, but by then Schneider had resigned as director over a disagreement with Bert Lahr, who had always considered himself 'the top banana' of the show and insisted on controlling the casting for the Broadway transfer. When the play opened in New York (at the John Golden Theatre on 19 April 1956) Herbert Berghof directed Bert Lahr in his Miami role but otherwise with a changed cast. As in London, press reaction was on the whole tepid, if not frankly derisive, perhaps partly because the Miami fiasco induced the New York advertisers to over-compensate by stressing that the play was for intellectuals only. But one or two prominent writers sprang to its defence: Eric Bentley, writing in *New Republic* on 14 May 1956, insisted that his colleagues had dismissed an 'important play', a 'rich piece of writing'. And Norman Mailer, whose initial reaction had been that *Godot* 'was a poem to impotence' calculated to appeal only to the impotent, took the unusually honest and courageous step of buying public advertising space in the paper in which he had originally reviewed the work, and which he had in the interval quarrelled with and left, to issue a recantation prompted by a closer study of the play. 'For an artist to attack another', he declared, 'and to do it on impulse, is a crime, and for the first time in months I have been walking around with a very clear sense of guilt' (*Village Voice*, 7 May 1956). Mailer's revised view is characteristically idiosyncratic (he sees the two clowns as 'a male and female homosexual, old and exhausted') but is forcefully and fairly put. A more sober and considered reaction came from William Barrett (*Saturday Review*, 8 June 1957): 'when I read *Waiting for Godot*', he wrote, 'I had that strangely simple and inevitable feeling that only a genuinely new work of art can produce', and attributed complaints about the play's 'obscurity' to the fact that 'what is so simple and central to some is terra incognita to others'.

But by this time the battle over Beckett's status as a dramatist had moved from newspaper offices to college campuses, where student directors took him up enthusiastically, and professors began turning the spotlight of their critical scholarship on the most hidden corners of his canon, with, as one might expect, unequal results. One of the first, and probably the best, of all scholarly discussions of Beckett's dramatic originality was published by Sorbonne professor Jean-Jacques Mayoux in *Etudes Anglaises* (October 1957). Mayoux stressed that in his 'great parody of theatre' Beckett recreates anew the sempiternal 'theatrical reality' of artistic truth: the truth about ourselves. Other academic responses were less felicitous. In his review of *The Theatre of Protest and Paradox* by George Wellwarth (*New Statesman*, 22

January 1965), the playwright John Mortimer singled out for scornful rebuttal a statement that '*what* Vladimir and Estragon do is not important at all'; on the contrary, replied Mortimer, '*what* Vladimir and Estragon do is of supreme importance: demonstrated by the minute and beautiful care with which the play is contrived'. Wellwarth's well-meant but misguided attempts to 'disregard the actual incidents of a play and apprehend instead the general theme of the author' fell foul, Mortimer argued, of the reality that in the work of an 'undoubted genius' like Beckett there is 'total lack of a general theme', merely 'an intense and painful individual expression'. Playwrights in general have, perhaps not surprisingly, been far more perceptive than most academics in discerning the precise nature of Beckett's theatrical achievement: Thornton Wilder, Alan Schneider tells us, 'considered *Godot* one of the two greatest modern plays', and in his 'Seven Notes on *Waiting for Godot*' (*Primer Acto*, April 1957), the Spanish dramatist Alfonso Sastre maintained that 'while we are left cold by many dramas of intrigue in which a great deal happens, this "nothing happens" of *Waiting for Godot* keeps us in suspense'. As for younger playwrights, Pinter has frequently declared his admiration (for instance in the festschrift *Beckett at Sixty*), and the extent of Tom Stoppard's debt in *Rosencrantz and Guildenstern are Dead* has been searchingly documented by Anthony Callen (*New Theatre Magazine*, Winter 1969).

This all-pervading influence of Beckett's language and imagery is nowhere more tellingly revealed than in the uses political cartoonists have put them to. During the last days of the Macmillan administration Vicky was inspired to depict the British Premier as Vladimir and one of his Cabinet colleagues as Estragon ruefully contemplating a newspaper headline about 'Budget Hopes' and declaring 'We'll hang ourselves tomorrow ... Unless Godot comes.' Truly, as Ronald Bryden saw in 1965, Beckett had 'become a climate of

opinion'; his tramps had not only gone round the world, they
had become part of contemporary mythology.

After such an apotheosis, it was to be expected that the
creation of *Endgame* (the work that gave rise to such critical
clichés of the time as 'dustbin philosophy' and 'ashcan drama')
would be something of an anticlimax. Beckett had begun
thinking about writing a new play in 1954, but only started
it in December 1955. At first it consisted of two Acts, but
since there was no aesthetic justification for a binary structure
as there had been in *Godot*, in revising his typescript Beckett
abolished the intermission and cut out other unsatisfactory
material to leave the longish one-acter we are familiar with.
The play gave him far more trouble than *Godot*: not until
October 1956 was Blin able to begin rehearsals, once again
without immediate hope of finding a theatre in which to put
it on. Since no Paris house could be persuaded to risk it,
Blin accepted the Royal Court's invitation to première the
play in London on 3 April 1957. Roger Blin himself created the
part of Hamm, Jean Martin was Clov, Georges Adet played
Nagg and Christine Tsingos, Nell. The well-intentioned
compromise of playing a new and difficult French play in
London was not a success: with characteristic wry humour,
Beckett described the occasion to Schneider as 'rather grim,
like playing to mahogany, or rather teak'. The fault cannot
however be said to lie entirely with an audience which of
necessity did not fully understand the language of the actors:
the production itself must bear part of the responsibility for
the semi-fiasco, being rather monotonous, shrill and dis-
jointed. Jacques Noel's décor consisted of a rather obvious
grey-green cave-like interior which added to the oppressive
effect. Clearly the actors were not at ease at the Royal Court,
nor in their parts, and a sort of resentment seemed to flow
back and fro across the footlights. When the short season
came to an end, Kenneth Tynan reacted forcibly: 'last week's
production, portentously stylized, piled on the agony until

I thought my skull would split' (*The Observer*, 7 April 1957). Harold Hobson was predictably enthusiastic and showed more discernment, but he overstated the case and passed over the fact that the production was marred by its hectoring manner. Beckett's collaborator in *Le Kid*, Georges Pelorson, writing under his usual pseudonym of Georges Belmont, declared in a 'London Letter' published in *Arts* (10 April 1957) that 'with *Fin de partie* Beckett has attained to classical perfection' but even he 'occasionally regretted a certain slowness and forced quality in Blin's delivery'. When the play transferred to the pocket Studio des Champs-Elysées on 26 April the Paris reviewers received the play with respect on the whole, but with little warmth. Some were actively hostile, notably the philosopher Gabriel Marcel, who in *Les Nouvelles Littéraires* (20 June 1957) declared that he had only been to see the play at the request of his readers, and as a result had spent one of the most painful evenings of his critical career due to the almost unbearable boredom and claustrophobia he suffered. Those with stronger nerves, like Maurice Nadeau (*France-Observateur*, 28 February 1957) admired Beckett's rigour in showing uncompromisingly the 'derision of the human condition'. But Nadeau was writing before the play's staging, on the basis of the published text which appeared in French in January, as was Beckett's old friend of Trinity days, A. J. Leventhal, who realized that '*Fin de partie* cannot hope for the same success that attended *Waiting for Godot* . . . an audience, faced with uttermost pain on the stage, is likely to wilt at the experience, though it may well be a catharsis for such who have hitherto refused in their euphoria to look beyond their optimistic noses' (*Dublin Magazine*, April 1957).

During the months after the creation of the French version, Beckett translated the play into English under the title *Endgame*, and Alan Schneider, who had been in touch with him throughout its development (their correspondence was published in the *Village Voice* on 19 March 1958) directed it at the Cherry Lane Theatre in New York on 28 January 1958, with P. J. Kelly and Nydia Westman as Nagg and Nell, and Lester Rawlins and Alvin Epstein as Hamm and Clov. Unlike Blin, Schneider did not set the play in a cavernous cell but used the dirty, bare back wall of the theatre as décor. Someone turned the central heating off before the curtain went up on the first night, causing the radiators as they cooled off to click loudly throughout the performance. The critics, and even Schneider's agent, assumed the noise was intended as part of the production, and praised the originality of the idea. As a result Schneider had to ensure that the unintended accompaniment was repeated on subsequent nights. The play was 'a significant off-Broadway success' according to John Unterecker (*New Leader*, 18 May 1959), designed for the playgoer who wants to be confronted with reality, but Schneider is wry about Beckett's critics. They begin, he says, by saluting Play A as 'awful'. When Play B comes along, that too is awful, and not nearly as good as A was. Play C is then dismissed as being awful, worse than B, which though good was not a patch on A, which in the interval has become a masterpiece. We have seen the retrospective whitewashing at work in the case of *Godot*, and the same applies to *Endgame*, which the *New York Daily News* gaily headlined as being 'Off-Broadway and Out of One Reviewer's Mind'. One of the sillier exegeses it threw up was Lionel Abel's to the effect that the play was autobiographical since Hamm clearly represented Joyce the father and Clov, Beckett the son (*New Leader*, 14 December 1959). Herbert Blau, however, who produced the play in San Francisco, made this characteristically perceptive comment on Hamm's yawn ('No, all is a – bsolute'): 'with that yawn, indifferent and cosmic, Hamm fractures the absolute. Before we accuse Beckett of rubbing despair in, we ought to hear the sough of history in that joke, the crossbreeding of satanic laugh and sonic boom' (*Encore*, September 1962).

Endgame (in English this time) returned to London and the Royal Court on 28 October 1958 in a double bill with *Krapp's Last Tape*. The director was the late George Devine, who also played Hamm, and Jack MacGowran took the part of Clov which he has since made his own. T. C. Worsley, however, was not impressed. He found it a relief to turn from 'the seamier side of Mr Beckett's nasty Unconscious' to the 'lucidity of Hauptmann's late nineteenth-century social conscience' (*New Statesman*, 8 November 1958), and Kenneth Tynan took solace in parody: '*Slamm's Last Knock*, a play inspired, if that is the word, by Samuel Beckett's double bill at the Royal Court,' which ends:

SLAMM. Is that all the review he's getting?
SECK. That's all the play he's written.

(*The Observer*, 2 November 1958)

Worsley's fastidious distaste and Tynan's not over-accurate pastiche were spiritedly and effectively demolished by Roy Walker writing in *The Twentieth Century* for December. Beckett cannot, he argued, be written off as a 'unique pathological oddity': his 'scathing satires on the sin and instability of man' must be seen as ranking 'among the greatest plays yet to appear upon the modern stage', for 'he has found in the depths of despair "the right kind of pity" for the individual and universal human condition of our time'. Walker stressed the Shakespearean overtones in *Endgame* (Hamm being a cross between Prospero and Richard III). The most thoroughgoing exploration of this particular theme was of course Jan Kott's controversial chapter on '*King Lear*, or Endgame' in *Shakespeare Our Contemporary* (1964): 'in both Shakespearean and Beckettian Endgames it is the modern world that fell; the Renaissance world, and ours'. Partial and selective as Kott's view is, it has the merit, in treating Shakespeare's plays as savage parables for our own age, of illuminating several parallels of mood and theme between them and Beckett's, suggesting incidentally that, all proportions kept, the latter may of all contemporary playwrights be the one who approaches nearest to Shakespearean universality and complex simplicity.

After the Royal Court run and the almost routine broadcasts by the ever-faithful BBC (both the French and English versions were heard on the Third Programme), *Endgame* was next seen in a major production in London in July 1964. Starring Patrick Magee as Hamm and MacGowran as Clov, it had already enjoyed a successful run in Paris. Once again Beckett was largely responsible for the direction, and critics were not slow to notice that in contrast to Blin's version it revealed a coarse and robust humour which made the whole livelier and more dramatic. J. W. Lambert spoke of 'Beckett's marvellous verbal mosaic . . . shot through with rueful comedy' (*Sunday Times*, 12 July 1964), and praise was unanimous for the Magee–MacGowran duo: 'they are consistently alert to each other's moods and project a relationship which is a mixture of reluctant affection and animosity, desperation and sullen dependence', wrote Peter Lennon in *The Guardian* (21 February 1964). Their interpretation seems to have come as close to the definitive as anything we are likely to see. *Endgame*, as Beckett admitted in his correspondence with Alan Schneider, is a difficult play to get right. Perhaps we should therefore recognize that initial critical resistance to the work was attributable in part to production teething troubles; or maybe it's quite simply easier for us to take the play now. Deliberately less rich (one might even say less baroque) than *Waiting for Godot*, it is arguably a greater achievement, with its Shakespearean and Strindbergian dimensions (Laurence Kitchin drew attention in *The Listener* of 24 January 1963 to a possible reminiscence of the fortress from *The Dance of Death*). 'A masterpiece of ambiguity' was Ross Chambers's description of Hamm's closing tirade (*Studi Francesi*, January 1967), but the term applies equally well to the whole of this dense and enigmatic work.

Of Beckett's two mime plays little needs to be said, or indeed has been said, although Irving Wardle allowed himself to be betrayed into something perilously like critic's guff when he praised Charles Marowitz's production of *Act Without Words II* at In-Stage in London for its 'strong surface humour and real sense of tragedy' (*The Observer*, 15 July 1962). Usually the mimes are performed as afterpieces (as for example by Deryk Mendel to music by the author's cousin John Beckett in the double bill *Fin de partie/Acte sans paroles I* at the Royal Court in 1957), or in anthology programmes compiled of various Beckett excerpts, such as the successful *End of Day* which Jack MacGowran presented single-handed at the London Arts Theatre in October 1962 after the Dublin Festival; and a short puppet film has even been made out of one of the mimes by Bruno and Guido Bettiol. Although Roy Walker (*The Listener*, 9 May 1957) claimed to have seen *Act Without Words I* 'precisely imagined by Bosch in a detail of the "Temptation of Saint Anthony"', Beckett himself seems to look upon the mimes (written in French between 1956 and 1958) as five-finger exercises. 'His interest', wrote Charles Marowitz in *Encore* (March 1962) after discussing them with him, 'is not so much in mime but in the stratum of movement which underlies the written word', and in productions with which he has been associated he attempts, Marowitz went on, to bring out the 'stylised movement' in accordance with which all his plays are structured.

All That Fall was written after the BBC had suggested to Beckett that he try his hand at radio drama. Its composition followed immediately on that of *Fin de partie*; it was broadcast by the BBC Third Programme on 13 January 1957 in a production by Donald McWhinnie with a largely Irish cast, including a great radio actress, the late Mary O'Farrell, in the role of Mrs Rooney, and Patrick Magee and Jack MacGowran in smaller parts. Roy Walker was predictably quick to proclaim the piece 'a radio classic' and rate it even higher than

Under Milk Wood: Beckett 'goes further', he wrote, 'in making the blind man's theatre of radio an art form in its own right' (*The Listener*, 24 January 1957). The poet Christopher Logue, writing in the *New Statesman* (14 September), used the phrase 'radio triumphant' in his review, which like Austin Clarke's in the *Irish Times* (7 September) drew attention to the comedy of the situation and sounds. Donald Davie (another poet), while stressing Beckett's originality in inducing syntax to 'parody itself', criticized the play as a whole for its 'derivative slapstick' and 'trick ending' (*Spectrum*, Winter 1958), but Hugh Kenner, as so often, put his finger on the real issue when he argued that 'radio proves to be the perfect medium for Beckett's primary concern: the relationship between words, silence and existence' (*Spectrum*, Spring 1961). The French translation was broadcast on Paris radio in December 1959 with Roger Blin as Mr Rooney, but created a far greater impact when (against the author's better judgement) it was televised in January 1963: 'ce fut admirable' exclaimed François Mauriac in the *Figaro Littéraire* (2 February), leading a chorus of praise from French reviewers.

Beckett's next radio play, *Embers* (broadcast by the BBC Third Programme on 24 June 1959), was awarded the Italia Prize for Donald McWhinnie's production with Jack Mac-Gowran in the main part, but attracted less critical attention. Fellow-playwright John Whiting praised 'a dramatic prose which has the precision of fine poetry' and the musical 'exactness' of the notation (*London Magazine*, May 1960), but Karl Miller reacted harshly, condemning 'technical weaknesses, boring repetitiveness, obscurity', and the whole 'pathetic and presumptuous' drift of Beckett's work and its lack of the 'means of control which art is supposed to need' (*Encounter*, September 1959). One wonders whether he, unlike Frank Kermode whose first reaction was also dismissive (*Encounter*, July 1960), has since maintained that view. The other radio works provoked steadily decreasing enthusiasm.

If the *Times* reviewer of *Words and Music*, broadcast by the BBC on 13 November 1962 with Patrick Magee in a production by Michael Bakewell to music by John Beckett, was characteristically respectful, Paul Ferris called it a 'hoarse and unsatisfactory assault on ideas that makes as little concession as possible to formal playwriting' (*The Observer*, 18 November). The last radio play to date, *Cascando*, was written in French and broadcast by the RTF on 13 October 1963 to a musical score by Marcel Mihalovici, whose 1961 operatic version of *Krapp's Last Tape* Beckett had admired. Roger Blin directed and played Opener, and Jean Martin was Voice. The BBC broadcast the English version a year later with Denys Hawthorne and Patrick Magee in a production by Donald McWhinnie. *The Listener*'s reviewer P. N. Furbank conceded that it would make little sense to anyone who had not followed the previous stages of Beckett's development, 'but then, isn't that rather unusual at the moment', he asked, 'to find an author whose development matters?' (15 October 1964). This 'work of genius', he went on, 'is about the impossibility of *not* writing, of not telling oneself stories'. Similarly appreciative was John Holmstrom: 'the flavour, the whole quality that makes his despair bearable and even lively, lies in the words, that inimitable partnership of misery, music hall and the English prose tradition' (*New Statesman*, 16 October 1964). Apart from giving rise to such scattered reactions as these, however, Beckett's radio drama seems to have slipped into an unobtrusive place in the canon.

The same cannot be said, fortunately, of the more recent stage plays. *Krapp's Last Tape*, for example, was early recognized as the minor dramatic masterpiece it is. It was written with a particular actor in mind, Patrick Magee: Beckett had been impressed by Magee's gritty readings of extracts from his fiction (*Molloy*, *Malone Dies*, *From an Abandoned Work*) broadcast on the BBC Third Programme around 1957, and the Irish actor duly created the part under Donald

McWhinnie's direction as the curtain-raiser in the double bill with *Endgame* at the Royal Court Theatre in London on 28 October 1958. In his December *Twentieth Century* review already referred to, Roy Walker saw that 'the soliloquy has found, for the first and probably the last time, a form which combines the immobile mask and the mobile face, mime and speech, monologue and dialogue, and offers all their various resources to one performer', and that 'future histories of the drama' will 'have something to say about it'. The play was premièred in New York at the Provincetown Playhouse (in a double bill with Albee's *The Zoo Story*) on 14 January 1960, starring Donald Davis directed by Alan Schneider, and Robert Brustein reviewed it enthusiastically as Beckett's 'best dramatic poem about the old age of the world', flawless and economical, haunting and harrowing (*New Republic*, 22 February 1960). The French translation was put on at the Récamier annex of the Théâtre National Populaire in Paris on 22 March 1960; R.-J. Chauffard played Krapp and Blin directed once again. Robert Kanters called it 'a kind of lyrical poem of solitude' (*L'Express*, 31 March), and fellow-critics were equally impressed. But as with other works, audiences had to wait for perfection until the author took more of a direct hand: his direction of Martin Held's Schiller Theater performance, recently seen in London, has rightly been hailed as definitive.

The volume of reaction to *Happy Days* was even greater than to *Krapp's Last Tape*, making it after *Godot* probably Beckett's most written-about play. The world première was at the Cherry Lane Theatre, New York, on 17 September 1961, with Ruth White as Winnie and John C. Becher as Willie, directed by Alan Schneider. The London *Times*'s special correspondent cabled home that upon a 'substructure of gloom, defeat and impotence, Mr Beckett has constructed a portrait of an incurable optimist . . . the dramatic situation puts her optimism into sharp contrast with the obvious hopelessness of her state' (25 September), but went on, somewhat inconsistently, to deny the play much theatrical quality. *Time*'s reviewer breezily reported that '*Happy Days* pursues the playwright's favourite thesis that life is slow death' (29 September), and only found Miss White's performance worthy of praise, a note struck by most of the journalistic critics. Even the well-disposed *Village Voice* found the play 'thinner in texture, slighter in consequence, than all its forerunners' (Jerry Talmer, 21 September). A more sympathetic reaction came from John Simon in the *Hudson Review* (Winter 1961–2): 'the play is full of that Beckettian strategy which presents the most innocuous trifles of human existence dripping with blood and bile, and the most unspeakable horrors rakishly attired and merrily winking'. Simon went on to make a point about the 'egregiously valid theatrical metaphor' constituted by Winnie's 'blithering about the great mercies of existence as she is pressed deeper and deeper into the sod', which was echoed by Peter Brook (*Encore*, January 1962): 'Beckett at his finest', wrote Brook, more in sorrow than in anger at *Happy Days*'s failure to surmount New York's indifference, 'seems to have the power of casting a stage picture, a stage relationship, a stage machine from his most intense experiences that in a flash, inspired, *exists*, stands there complete in itself, not *telling* not *dictating*, symbolic without symbolism.'

The play came to London in November 1962 (Brenda Bruce and Peter Duguid being directed by George Devine at the Royal Court), where it was better received. For *The Times* (3 November) 'the text is an elaborate structure of internal harmonies, with recurring clichés twisted into bitter truths, and key phrases chiming ironically through the development as in a passacaglia'. Bernard Levin declared that this 'terminus in the drama' would 'haunt those who see it'; Kenneth Tynan felt 'it is a dramatic metaphor extended beyond its capacities' but urged his readers to see it; and Harold Hobson, countering the notion that Beckett is a sentimentalist, argued that the play is about 'how one is happy because half-buried' and therefore calls 'for radiance, not heroism' on the part of its actress. The role was in fact more judiciously recreated by Marie Kean in Jack Mac-Gowran's production at London's Stratford East in December 1963.

The French translation came to the Paris Odéon via the Venice festival in October 1963 in a prestigious production by Roger Blin with Madeleine Renaud and Jean-Louis Barrault. From the outset the self-conscious 'star' treatment of the parts imposed respect on the critics, but it probably did the play a disservice: Madeleine Renaud was, one might say, magnificently miscast. Beckett's derision of all theatre hardly had a chance in the hands of such a great professional: one could not resist the sacrilegious thought that she would have coped with, say, the failure of the parasol to explode at the correct moment in the first Act as serenely as she surmounted the indignities of gesture and posture imposed on her by the stage directions. The Paris critics at least did not measure their praises: '*inoubliable*' said Jacques Lemarchand, '*sublime*', echoed Bertrand Poirot-Delpech, '*admirable*' gasped Claude Sarraute. One wonders what such critics would have said if an *inconnue* had created the part, or even if they had known that Beckett decided originally to make the role a female one simply because a shopping-bag gave him more scope for humorous business than the contents of a man's trouser pockets would have done. . . .

Play was created in German translation at Ulm on 14 June 1963, with Nancy Illig, Sigrid Pfeiffer and Gerhard Winter in a production by Deryk Mendel, who performed the two *Acts Without Words* on the same occasion. Alan Schneider premièred the original English text at the Cherry Lane Theatre, New York, on 4 January 1964, with Frances Sternhagen, Marian Reardon and Michael Lipton, and London's National Theatre followed suit with George Devine directing Rosemary Harris, Billie Whitelaw and Robert Stephens on 7 April 1964. Once again Beckett had created an original and arresting dramatic metaphor: but the London *Times*'s correspondent in Ulm (24 June 1963) saw only a 'depressing no-man's-land of the after-life'. Barbara Bray, more perceptively, noted 'Beckett's inventiveness, formal mastery and poetic power' (*The Observer*, 16 June). Reviewing the London production, Harold Hobson (*Sunday Times*, 12 April 1964) appreciated the *da capo* repetition with characteristic acuteness: 'all in the story that had seemed vague becomes sharp and clear. The incidents stand out: only the emotions – the sadness, the compassion, and the pain – are still beyond computation.' Perhaps the play communicated (suggested Laurence Kitchin in *The Listener*, 30 April) at a subliminal level like 'tightly compressed chamber music'. No such praise from the *Times Educational Supplement* (15 May), for whom the play made only 'an amusing technical exercise'. For Bamber Gascoigne (*The Observer*, 12 April), it was merely a further stage in 'the gradual desiccation and boxing-in' for which Beckett's theatre is notorious, and the *Daily Express* felt impelled to headline Herbert Kretzmer's notice (8 April) as 'The Three Faces of Beckett's Contempt'.

When Jean-Marie Serreau created the French version at the Pavillon de Marsan, Paris, on 11 June 1964, with three remarkable performers (Delphine Seyrig, Eléonore Hirt and Michael Lonsdale), even Pierre-Aimé Touchard, who in February 1961 had contributed a fine essay on Beckett's theatre to the *Revue de Paris*, voiced his disquiet at what he felt was a growing tendency towards a minority esotericism (*Le Monde*, 1 December 1964). As for the production's filmed version, made with the assistance of Marin Karmitz, Jean Ravel and Beckett himself, this was 'annihilated with derisory applause' at the Venice Festival, according to Dilys Powell (*Sunday Times*, 4 September 1966).

Beckett's work conceived in 1963 directly for the cinema,

Film, was made in the heat of a New York July, during his only visit to that city in 1964. Alan Schneider was the director, and Beckett suggested Buster Keaton (who died not long after) for the main part, thereby repaying a long-standing debt to one of the masters of silent comedy. *Film* won awards at Venice and Tours, but elicited from veteran film critic Dilys Powell the comment 'personally I think *Film* is a load of old bosh' (*Sunday Times*, 21 November 1965), which Roy Walker had wittily forestalled seven years previously when he had said 'there is more Bosch than bosh about Beckett'. More piously, the British magazine *Film* (Winter 1965–6) spoke of 'a strange and haunting experience' provoked by 'a work more closely approximating to the definition of film as an art than we have seen for a long time'. Raymond Federman's considered opinion was that this movie used as its subject film's own essence, 'visual perception', and that its purpose was 'to show the ambiguity of perception, which is shared both by the perceiver and that which is perceived' (*Film Quarterly*, Winter 1966–7).

The 'story' of *Film*, which Federman rightly argues is 'trivial, almost irrelevant', has something in common not only with *Krapp's Last Tape* but also with the television play *Eh Joe*, written in 1965 and broadcast by the BBC on 4 July 1966, with Jack MacGowran and Sian Phillips in a production by Michael Bakewell, assisted by the author. J. C. Trewin found it a 'lugubrious experience' and criticized the scale of the work as 'almost excessively small' (*The Listener*, 21 July).

Of *Come and Go* and *Breath* there is – not unnaturally – little to say. The first, puckishly subtitled 'dramaticule', is dedicated to Beckett's British publisher John Calder: like *Play*, it was premièred in German by Deryk Mendel, this time at the Berlin Schiller Theater with Lieselotte Rau, Charlotte Joeres and Sibylle Gilles in September 1965. A few months later Beckett himself put on the French version at the Odéon with Madeleine Renaud, Annie Bertin and

Simone Valère. It was performed in English at the Oxford Playhouse on 8 March 1970 as part of a Beckett evening in aid of the Samuel Beckett Theatre Appeal, as was *Breath*, originally written in response to Kenneth Tynan's request for a contribution to his Broadway review *Oh! Calcutta*, but withdrawn from the London transfer because of Tynan's alleged failure either to respect Beckett's stage directions (which make no provision for the naked bodies that lent a rather different significance to the 'breath'), or to attribute the contribution to its author by name. Even so, Raymond Williams was, predictably enough, not impressed by the Oxford production, preferring to Beckett's respiratory shorthand 'one of the other life-sounds: a belly laugh' (*The Listener*, 19 March 1970).

We must not forget, however, that true to Alan Schneider's wry description of the critical process, these derisive pleasantries about the recent works were uttered at the same time (and often by the same people) as the fulsome accolades bestowing classical status upon the past canon, on the laurels of which, we are lectured, the author (unlike some of his *confrères*) is perversely reluctant to recline. One cannot win, it would appear: either one is admonished by one's critics for not renewing oneself, or one is blamed for trying to avoid settling into a rut.

But I should not like this tawdry observation to emerge as the sole conclusion to the story of performances of Beckett's plays and of responses to them that I have been tracing in this chapter. Alongside much flippant and unhelpful commentary (the bulk of which, of course, I have left undisturbed in its files) there are, as I have tried to show, the essays that stand out long afterwards as examples of sympathetic and enlightening criticism. I have hardly mentioned German reviews, either, and yet writers like Gerda Zeltner-Neukomm of the *Neue Zürcher Zeitung* have a distinguished record in this respect. The Scandinavians, too, have accorded Beckett a cordial reception on the whole, as have certain Italian critics. But to chronicle their reactions would have inflated the material beyond bounds without affecting substantially the overall picture, which is likely to remain much the same in the future. The Nobel prizewinner's past work will, by its very nature, attain increasingly to the status of a monument of European dramaturgy, while his austere attempts not to be cast in the role of a grand old man of twentieth-century letters will continue to be met with baffled disappointment by those whose profession it should be to welcome such vitality, but who, all too often, show a peevish kind of resentment over the obvious fact that no artist worthy of the name (think of Ibsen, or Matisse) is ever truly classifiable during his own lifetime.

" WE'LL HANG OURSELVES TO MORROW" (HE PAUSES) "UNLESS GODOT COMES."
— WAITING FOR GODOT, ACT II

Bibliographical Note

1 EDITIONS CITED

(a) PLAYS

All That Fall. London: Faber & Faber, 1957.

Breath. *Gambit*, IV, 16 (1970), pp. 8–9.

Come and Go. London: Calder & Boyars, 1967.

Eh Joe, Act Without Words II, Film. London: Faber & Faber, 1967.

Endgame and Act Without Words I. London: Faber & Faber, 1958.

Happy Days. London: Faber & Faber, 1962.

Krapp's Last Tape and Embers. London: Faber & Faber, 1959.

Play, Words and Music, Cascando. London: Faber & Faber, 1967.

Waiting for Godot. London: Faber & Faber, 1965.

(b) OTHER WORKS

'Beckett's Letters on *Endgame*'. *Village Voice*, 19 March 1958, pp. 8, 15.

'Dante . . . Bruno . Vico . . Joyce', in *Our Exagmination Round His Factification for Incamination of Work in Progress*. New York: New Directions, 1962.

How It Is. London: Calder & Boyars, 1964.

More Pricks Than Kicks. London: Calder & Boyars, 1970.

Murphy. London: Calder & Boyars, 1963.

No's Knife. London: Calder & Boyars, 1967.

Poems in English. London: Calder & Boyars, 1961.

Proust and Three Dialogues with Georges Duthuit. London: Calder & Boyars, 1965.

Three Novels (*Molloy, Malone Dies, The Unnamable*). London: Calder & Boyars, 1959.

Watt. London: Calder & Boyars, 1963.

2 OTHER BOOKS AND PERIODICALS CONSULTED

BABLET, Denis. *Edward Gordon Craig* (tr. Daphne Woodward). London: Heinemann, 1966.

BENEDIKT, Michael and George E. Wellwarth, eds. and trs. *Modern French Plays.* London: Faber & Faber, 1965.

BENTLEY, Eric, ed. *The Theory of the Modern Stage.* Harmondsworth: Penguin Books, 1968.

BRANCUSI, Constantin. Quoted in *Catalogue of Brancusi Exhibition.* The Hague: Gemeentemuseum, 1970.

BRAUN, Edward, tr. and ed. *Meyerhold on Theatre.* London: Methuen, 1969.

CALDER, John, ed. *Beckett at Sixty.* London: Calder & Boyars, 1967.

COHN, Ruby, ed. *Casebook on 'Waiting for Godot'.* New York: Grove Press, 1967.

COHN, Ruby, ed. *Modern Drama* (Samuel Beckett Issue), IX, 3 (December 1966).

DRIVER, Tom F. 'Beckett by the Madeleine'. *Columbia University Forum,* IV (Summer 1961), pp. 21–5.

DUCKWORTH, Colin, ed. *En attendant Godot.* London: Harrap, 1966.

GLENAVY, Beatrice Lady. *Today We Will Only Gossip.* London: Constable, 1964.

HAYMAN, Ronald. Interview with Martin Held. *Times Saturday Review,* 25 April 1970.

JANVIER, Ludovic. *Samuel Beckett par lui-même.* Paris: Seuil, 1969.

KNOWLSON, James. *Catalogue of Samuel Beckett Exhibition.* London: Turret Books, 1971.

MÉLÈSE, Pierre. *Beckett.* Paris: Seghers, 1966.

REID, Alec. *All I Can Manage, More Than I Could.* Dublin: Dolmen Press, 1968.

SHENKER, Israel. 'Moody Man of Letters'. *New York Times,* 6 May 1956.

SMITH, B. C. *Some Features of the Dramatic Language of Samuel Beckett.* Unpublished B.Ed. Dissertation, University of Birmingham, 1970.

STOUT, A. K., ed. *Aspects of Drama and the Theatre.* Sydney: University Press, 1965.

WINDSOR, Duke of. Interview with Kenneth Harris. *The Listener,* 15 January 1970.

YATES, Frances A. *The Art of Memory.* London: Routledge & Kegan Paul, 1966; repr. Penguin Books, 1969.

This list is strictly selective. For a full bibliography the reader is referred to *Samuel Beckett, His Works and His Critics: An Essay in Bibliography* by Raymond Federman and John Fletcher, University of California Press, 1970.

NOTE—In the United States, Grove Press has published the following works by Beckett: *Cascando* (1969), *Collected Works,* 16 vols. (1970), *Endgame* (1958), *Film, a Film Script* (1969), *Happy Days* (1961), *How It Is* (1964), *Krapp's Last Tape and Other Dramatic Pieces* (1960), *Murphy* (1967), *Poems in English* (1963), *Proust* (1958), *Stories and Texts for Nothing* (1967), *Three Novels* (1965), *Waiting for Godot* (1966), and *Watt* (1959).

Index